MW01284278

UNBREAKABLE VALOR

TRIUMPH THROUGH THE SOUL OF RESILIENCE!

SHAUN L. MURPHY

13TH & JOAN

Unbreakable Valor: Triumph through the Soul of Resilience!
Copyright 2024 by Shaun L. Murphy.

All rights reserved. No part of this publication may be
reproduced, distributed, or transmitted in any form or by
any means, including photocopying, recording, or other
electronic or mechanical methods, without the prior
written permission of the publisher, except in the case of
brief quotations embodied in critical reviews and certain
other noncommercial uses permitted by copyright law.

For permission requests, write to the publisher, addressed
"Attention: Permissions Coordinator," 205 N. Michigan
Avenue, Suite #810, Chicago, IL 60601. 13th & Joan
books may be purchased for educational, business or
sales promotional use. For information, please email
the Sales Department at sales@13thandjoan.com.

Printed in the U. S. A.

First Printing, October 2024

Library of Congress Cataloging-in-
Publication Data has been applied for.

ISBN: 978-1-961863-07-1

DEDICATION

This book is dedicated to:

My spiritual father, for I am his baby boy and because of Him I can do all things!

Wifey, your unconditional love and continuous support, fuels me. V-Reign & Max, my reasons, my WHY, my everything!

Sis-tahhhh… four years my junior, and I've learned so much from you. You are my doubter & cheerleader morphed into one. You've always been there for me and I appreciate you!

My big bro, KC… Thanks for keeping that promise you made in my mom's crib.

To friends who I've connected with along the journey.

To my readers who are going through a tough time, there is light ahead of this tunnel.

Charlie… Di Ticklah smiling broad Iyah; #MyAce

All that I am and all that I ever will be, I owe to my prayer warrior, my hero, mom dukes, Sis Sis aka Sylvia Murphy! #Love

Table of Contents

Most people will experience a traumatizing event at some point in their lives. But when you add up all the statistics about traumatic events such as sexual abuse, violent crime, wartime experiences or natural disasters like Hurricane Katrina, it is clear that these acts of terror are an important public health matter.

If that is something you have gone through or you know someone who has been through this, then this book is for you. This will help people to learn how to process things.

Introduction

Strength (resilience) is within you. No matter your circumstance, how you grew up, your genetic composition, what is within you is greater than your story (excuses). In this book, you will discover aspects of yourself buried deep within your subconscious. You will tap into an energy source greater than the physical manifestation of what you think you are today. You will learn how to connect your divinity with your day-to-day persona and manifest the attributes you've always aspired to. Make the decision to park any doubt you may have about fully attaining a life filled with joy and walk away without looking back.

So many people are suffering in today's world. Comparison is all around us through social media, television, and the way we live in this modern age. Mental illness is on the rise as is anti-anxiety treatment plus medication. There is no need to feel frustrated or weighed down by the world around us. There is a shift happening and there are new techniques and strategies available to rewire your conscious and subconscious mind for success.

What would you do if you knew you could not lose? How would you move in the world? Well, this book is here to tell you that you get as much out of life from your losses as you do from your wins. You have to open your mind and eyes to raise your awareness of the message buried deep in the lesson. It's about changing your focus and starting anything how you want to finish. You are a highly organized organism and within you is the power to design your life into exactly what you've ever desired it to be. This is an absolute truth.

There is a solution to every problem and a sure way out of the maze of negative thought patterns.

CHAPTER 1

WHAT IS RESILIENCY?

Resiliency is defined as the capacity to recover quickly from difficulties; toughness. Resiliency is the process of adapting well in the face of adversity, trauma, tragedy, threats, or significant source of stress! As a collective people, we have an appreciation for toughness, but most of us shy away from the challenges that get us to that state.

The word "resiliency" is rooted in the Latin word resilire, which means to jump back. When applied to human beings, resiliency refers to the ability of individuals or communities exposed to high levels of stress and adversity to recover quickly from injury or trauma. Tenacity can be seen as an adaptation process that enables us not only to bounce back, but also adjust our outlooks and actions so that they are consistent with what is most important for us over time. We build grit when we have strong connections—to people who care about us, meaningful activities outside work (for example), a sense of being part of something larger than ourselves; when we feel competent at tasks relevant for our lives; and especially when we feel we have control over our actions.

Resiliency is like a muscle. The more we exercise it the stronger and healthier it becomes. When we don't use this capacity for adaptation or adjustment very much (or at all), or when we rely on others to take care of us instead of taking action ourselves, grit weakens and can even disappear completely. On average, people in Western societies show declining levels of grit as they age; indeed, one study concluded that college students today are less resilient than their counterparts were two decades ago—a trend further supported by another report showing that contemporary young adults experience higher rates of mental health problems than youth in any other time in recent history.

▆ WHY DOES IT MATTER?

This matters because it helps us survive and thrive in the face of adversity, stress, or trauma; we need to be able to bounce back from disappointments and move forward with our lives. Resilient people tend to experience happier moods and fewer negative views toward themselves, their families, and their communities than those who lack tenacity—and they may also recover more quickly when faced with physical illness or injury. In addition, research shows that resilient children are better at regulating emotions such as anger (which can help them avoid becoming bullies), while non-resilient kids often end up being aggressive on the playground due to frustration over not being able to control certain situations. This is particularly significant given how many studies have shown a link between bullying and later-life behavioral problems.

Finally, resilient people tend to be more successful in their careers than those who lack resiliency—and they are also better able to cope with workplace challenges such as change or conflicts that arise between employees and supervisors. These benefits may not only improve the work environment, but can help individuals perform better on the job by increasing productivity levels and reducing mistakes at work.

■ HOW CAN IT HELP YOU IN YOUR LIFE?

There are people who come from low-income communities, better known as the hood, who tend to be hardened with resilience. Their lived experiences make up the definition. Having endured trauma, tragedy, threats, or significant sources of stress is the fabric of their day-to-day lives in the hood.

Resiliency is something that can be learned, so even if you don't consider yourself to be particularly tough or strong now, developing tenaciousness could help you down the road. It's also important to understand why people experience high levels of resiliency—and this is about more than just having brawn and toughness.

Resilience is a survival mechanism for some. Think about those who are a product of low-income communities, they tend to be hardened with resilience. Having endured trauma, tragedy, threats, and or significant sources of stress; that's everyday life in the hood.

After researching successful individuals in various fields who have persevered through adversity (including Mother Teresa, Oprah Winfrey, and Maya Angelou), psychologist Karen Reivich has identified seven key attitudes toward life among those with resilient spirits: hope for the future; optimism; a sense of personal control over one's actions; self-efficacy (confidence in our ability to master new tasks); a capacity to find meaning in difficult situations; a sense of strong social support from family and friends, and commitment—the dedication that makes all else possible.

Resiliency is not just about survival in the face of difficulties but also thriving in their wake. Reivich has identified three key attitudes toward life among those who have thrived after experiencing tragedy or trauma: hope for the future (as mentioned above); positive reframing—looking at one's situation through a different lens to gain new insights into how things can be improved; building on existing strengths instead of focusing exclusively on what went wrong. Resilient people can constructively transform painful experiences into lessons they carry with them going forward rather than letting them hold them back.

WHAT ARE THE BENEFITS OF BEING RESILIENT?

Resiliency is not just for those going through a crisis but for anyone who wants to live a meaningful and fulfilling life. Tenacity does not have to be limited only to the extremes of trauma or tragedy. It can also help us handle everyday stress with greater ease and effectiveness, which ultimately helps create a better quality of life.

Benefits include:

- A resilient person manages stress better than other people; has strong coping skills that allow him/her to deal effectively with distressful situations such as loss or failure (and bounce back quickly).

- A resilient person is more optimistic about his/her future because he/she believes they will find ways out of their problems rather than feeling overwhelmed by them; takes responsibility for both good things and bad things.

- Job satisfaction increases by 30% according to a study done at the University of Illinois. This is because they are more likely to succeed in their jobs due to being resilient.

- People who are resilient and optimistic seem to be healthier than those people who aren't. Their immune system is stronger and they could recover from any illness faster even if their environment was constantly changing instead of staying in one place or with the same group of people.

- Resilient students do well academically because they know that past failures don't determine future ones so there's still a chance to succeed! Grit can give them hope for success after every failure.

- Resilient people bounce back quickly from disappointments and recover more rapidly from traumatic events. Tenacity helps you to see hope even when it's hard to because you know that no matter what, things could always be worse!

- A resilient person is someone who stays calm during a crisis instead of becoming confused or overwhelmed by the problem; takes responsibility for their actions rather than blaming others, which leads them to take appropriate action to solve problems.

- Reduced stress levels due to increased optimism about how future events will play out for them based on previous experiences with similar situations. This causes less anxiety-provoking thoughts leading these individuals towards better mental health outcomes overall. Stress can often create feelings of hopelessness, helplessness, and even depression.

- Better coping skills in times of crisis because they don't blame others for their problems; instead, they take responsibility. This leads to better problem-solving abilities, which often results in a more effective resolution or solution that most people would not have thought of otherwise.

- Mental health issues such as PTSD (Post-Traumatic Stress Disorder) are connected with an increased sense of learned helplessness due to past events leading to the belief that there's nothing you can do about it! Resilient individuals can move forward from traumatic experiences and see them as opportunities rather than burdens. Doing so puts less stress on your mind and body causing improved overall wellbeing physically and emotionally over time.

- Improved academic performance because they don't fear failure. They know that failure is a part of life and it's not going to stop them from being successful in the future! Academic success has been shown to increase grit, which leads students down a path towards better mental health, happiness, and overall wellbeing.

- A person who becomes resilient after experiencing great stress or trauma doesn't get stuck on their emotions but instead learns how to move forward from what happened; takes ownership over what he/she can change rather than feeling helpless about things outside his control.

HOW TO DEVELOP A SPIRIT OF RESILIENCY

People fail to develop the spirit of resiliency because they are either too afraid or do not give themselves enough time to grieve. Everyone develops a sense of resiliency by experiencing different challenges in their lives.

1. People who are spiritually grounded can be more resilient than others, which is why it is crucial to maintain this connection with God throughout life's circumstances. A connection with God provides wisdom, guidance, and most importantly hope; this hope allows people to keep pushing through the tough times so that they may one day look back on their experiences as lessons learned

rather than obstacles passed up. Other aspects of spirituality include developing an optimistic outlook on life by practicing gratitude for all that you have been and trusting in your faith that things will all work out as they should.

2. To develop tenaciousness one must be willing to deal with the uncomfortable, which is any challenge that arises in life. Many people avoid these challenges because they want to maintain their current state or situation. Unfortunately, avoiding these problems will only cause them to fester and grow until there is no other option but to address them directly.

3. A third tip for developing a spirit of tenaciousness comes from being honest with yourself about what you need from others and learning how to ask for it. When you can communicate your needs, you can trust that those around you will fulfill them without feeling abandoned or isolated. In addition, by asking for what you need you are also teaching others how to be supportive in ways that are comfortable for you.

4. One must learn when it is necessary to cut ties with people who no longer serve their purpose or add value to their lives. This can be difficult because oftentimes the relationships we have are built out of necessity rather than wanted connections. The truth is your life will only become more difficult if you feel obligated to continue these toxic relationships. Eventually, it becomes exhausting

and draining on your energy levels, which makes accomplishing other tasks impossible.

5. Developing a spirit of tenacity means being able to set boundaries with others so that everyone feels safe within the relationship. This will allow you to feel more confident in your interactions while also allowing others the freedom they need to be themselves. By setting boundaries with people, you are communicating that it is safe for them to be who they are around you because oftentimes this self-expression will only strengthen the relationship between both parties.

6. When someone else insults or criticizes you, never respond right away. Take a little time to think about what just happened and why it hurt so much. You may have heard something similar before so did you ignore it before? Did the other person have power over your choices in life? Or do they continue to do so? Whatever it is, after thinking things through, you can choose not to internalize these negative thoughts and instead use them as a steppingstone to become stronger and more resilient than before.

7. A tip for anyone looking to develop tenaciousness is to stay positive! Every day we wake up knowing that no matter what challenges we face, we will make it through! To accomplish this, it's important not to dwell on the negative aspect of life because even just one bad event can bring down your whole mood. Those who are optimistic tend to

find solutions to any given problem whereas those who are pessimistic take longer because they have given up hope from the beginning.

8. Find where you draw inspiration from during hard times. It could be a person, a song, a quote, or simply the sun rising in the morning, which gives you a renewed sense of energy to keep going. Whatever you draw inspiration from, you must choose something to bring comfort and remind yourself of your purpose in life!

Several factors are likely to influence the development of tenaciousness in an individual. Some of these include the following:

- Family dynamics, relationships, and support system
- Individual's perception of self-value and worthiness
- Prior life experiences
- Cultural environment and social expectations

All these factors play a role in influencing the level of tenacity an individual possesses, but it is also important to realize that everyone has the potential for developing tenacity even though certain obstacles may come up along the way. Grit can be developed through practical efforts by taking small steps towards meeting personal goals or overcoming challenges faced head-on. One effective tool would be learning how to reframe one's perspective on events that are not always negative as perceived initially upon experience without judgmental thinking patterns. This means opening up to new possibilities and opportunities when things seem bleak and difficult at first glance; something we could learn from children who often find joy amidst hardship and struggle. Another important step towards developing tenacity would be cultivating the ability to adapt, which is often easier said than done, especially under intense pressure and the uncertainty of life events that are beyond our control.

Learning how to develop better coping mechanisms in times of stress or crisis can also help build tenacity by strengthening an individual's emotional intelligence skills. This means understanding one's strengths and weaknesses while building on them with a positive approach towards change through self-reflection practices, finding support groups among family members or friends who offer encouragement during difficult times, learning more about what it takes to manage expectations of oneself as well as others around us, having faith in something bigger than ourselves even amidst loss/failure/suffering, etc., and finding a sense of purpose in whatever we do with our lives.

To develop a spirit of tenacity is to learn how to cope better amidst the challenges and setbacks that life has to offer while being able to stay focused on what makes us happy, fulfilled, or content even during difficult times. There are many paths towards achieving this goal, which means having an open mind and willing heart, understanding it requires effort from all parties involved but always remembering that tenacity can be learned through practical steps taken one step at a time rather than looking for someone else's way out of pain/suffering, etc. because ultimately everyone needs their individualized approach towards recovery within themselves first before helping others around them recover too. There Is Power in Developing a Spirit of Tenacity.

DO YOU THINK IT MATTERS IN TODAY'S SOCIETY?

Tenacity is more important now than ever before. Life seems to be getting harder and faster, especially for those with children or who are responsible for others like aging parents. The need to bounce back from the daily grind of life is becoming increasingly necessary as we face new challenges in our world today, some that were unheard of five years ago! We're also seeing an increase in suicides, drug abuse, and homelessness at rates not seen since World War II veterans returned home after serving their country. All this tells us one thing—grit matters.

CHAPTER 2

WHO DEALT THESE CARDS?

*The beginning of trauma
and its manifestations*

Thinking, *Why Me?* consciously or subconsciously is probably one of the most detrimental forms of self-sabotage we can exhibit. Traumatic episodes carry within them a seed. A seed that can produce positive results if we adapt by adopting and using the experiences to bolster our vision of what we aspire to be.

It is important to note that we should not look at traumatic moments as blessings; however, understanding the lessons and opportunities hidden within these experiences can be a great source of empowerment. The first step is to understand the types of conditions that create episodes of mental duress.

The following are potential causes of traumatic episodes or life-changing experiences, which can be either planned or spontaneous:

- Death of a loved one
- Loss of employment
- Injury/Illness

Even though these experiences are seen as negative for the majority who experience them, they can be used as opportunities to reboot our vision for ourselves. This often requires us to re-evaluate what we thought was important before and take into account how our lives have changed in both direction and speed. Without this introspective internal assessment, it becomes much harder to recover from trauma. We tend to think about things too literally without considering the changes in plans, schedules, and other constricting factors.

RATIONALIZING THE EXPERIENCE

Developing tenacity does not mean that we should rationalize or expect traumatic experiences to happen to us. It means that when they do, we find the good in them and become better for having gone through these trials.

Resilience is one of those words that elicit strong responses because, by definition, "tenacity is the capacity of a strained body to recover its size and shape after deformation caused especially by compressive stress." What we need to understand about this definition is that it only deals with physicality.

The true essence of tenacity has far-reaching effects and can take us from surviving life's adversities to thriving.

When we are faced with a traumatic event, our survival instincts can be so strong that they prevent us from moving on and progressing through the situation. Our minds become fixated on how unfair it is and we feel sorry for ourselves instead of looking at tenacity as a positive force in our lives.

WHAT IS TRAUMA AND WHAT ARE ITS EFFECTS?

Due to the nature of traumatic experiences, we may feel a sense of loss and betrayal. We begin to question ourselves and blame others for our misfortunes.

Trauma is defined as an emotional shock that creates disorder. It fundamentally changes the way we think about ourselves, other people, and the world. Extreme or overwhelming stress is required to induce trauma.

Trauma is impactful enough that it can paralyze us from moving on with our lives because we are stuck in its negative emotions like anger, fear, depression, anxiety, etc. What it does is create psychological gaps within us where we shut down or withdraw. When this happens, life becomes monotonous at best and miserable at worst.

The effects of trauma are usually lasting because it not only assaults our psyche but also attacks our spirit if we let it. Our psyche can be healed with time and introspection, but unless there are conscious efforts to look at the situation in a positive light, tenacity will never take root because there will always be something for us to focus on negatively—the absence of support from others when it happened, the fact that "it" occurred because someone did not do their job properly.

THE POWER OF TENACITY

So, if that is what trauma does to us, how do we reverse the process? Grit is not something you are born with. It is not a talent. It is a skill that can be learned by anyone willing to put forth the effort and time needed to cultivate it. At its core, tenacity gives us back our lives so we can live them fully instead of stagnantly trying to outrun our pasts.

It has been theorized that grit comes from inner strength, spiritual connectedness, supportive relationships, psychological coping skills, experiencing success at least once in life, and positive worldviews among others. The good news is that no matter who you are or where you come from, you can learn how to increase your resiliency.

WHAT ARE ITS FORMS?

The different forms that trauma can take are often misdiagnosed. Usually, it is assumed to be post-traumatic stress disorder (PTSD). PTSD is one of its manifestations since it is "a mental health problem that some people develop after experiencing or witnessing a life-threatening event like combat, disaster, or sexual assault," but what most people do not realize is that there are different types of traumas with varying effects. The important thing to remember is that trauma is not just a single event. It is the constant bombardment of stressors or any situation that makes us feel victimized or powerless in some way. Grit has to be nurtured and developed over time because otherwise we develop PTSD, which can seriously impact our lives—physically, emotionally, and spiritually; we lose sight of who we are and all we used to believe in.

WHAT HAPPENS IF IT GOES UNCHECKED?

If left unhealed, trauma eats away at our souls until there's nothing left but an empty shell wandering through the world trying desperately to hold on to anything that reminds them they were once alive. Eventually, life becomes monotonous at best and miserable at worst.

Trauma is a word we throw around casually without fully understanding it. It can range from something as traumatic as witnessing your sister die to something as common as quitting your job and looking for another one. The worst part about trauma is that it's usually unexpected and unknown until days, months, or even years later when it begins to fester and manifest itself in ways we least expect.

Most of us have been through trauma at some point in our lives. We've all experienced loss but some haven't been able to properly process the grief they felt at losing a loved one, a breakup, or even the loss of a pet. They might turn to substance abuse or, worse, depression. When this happens over an extended time, it can leave a permanent scar on their psyche.

What happens when you refuse to acknowledge it?

Unfortunately, the worst thing someone can do is try to suppress or ignore their trauma. We have this belief that we need to be strong to feel good about ourselves. If you're going through a period of extreme stress at work, chances are your friends won't reach out because they don't want to bother you even though they know what's been happening behind closed doors. You might also find yourself thinking you're fine from time to time even though your brain doesn't quite agree with the surface-level façade you've been trying so desperately to keep up. This is what it means to have a spirit of resiliency—the ability to feel something and then move on from that feeling.

The power of developing tenaciousness is all about being able to recognize your feelings without letting them dictate how you see the world. It's about acknowledging those feelings as they appear before they swallow you whole and refuse to spit you out until way after they're done with you. Everyone experiences some form of trauma whether they choose to ignore it or not, but those who've learned how to accept what happened without allowing it to take control over their lives are the ones reaping all the benefits.

▮ WHY INTROSPECTION MATTERS

Retrospective introspection matters because the difference between failure and success lies in how we look at our experiences. Our reactions to them determine how traumatic events will affect us—emotionally and psychologically—for the rest of our lives. As Socrates said, "The unexamined life is not worth living."

LEARNING ABOUT OUR FEARS IS THE BEST WAY TO GET OVER THEM

Fear is one of the most primal instincts in humans, so overcoming it requires some understanding of what causes it. Common responses include palpitations, paleness of skin or flushed cheeks, "butterflies" in the stomach, shaking and trembling, etc. Those who have experienced trauma may also feel disassociated from reality because all they can think about is their emotions, which overwhelms them even more. Be that as it may, there are ways to overcome fear by recognizing its triggers and taking steps to handle them instead of being paralyzed by anxiety when these symptoms occur. This type of introspection is how we get to the root of our fear and eventually overcome it. I have to thank one of my virtual mentors, Tim Ferris, for introducing me to fear setting. He has a Ted Talk I want you to check out called, "Why Should You Define Your Fears Instead of Goals," where it talks about a unique strategy.

A strategy that you can use to approach dealing with fear is to, instead of goal setting, try fear setting.

Define:
List out all of the worst things you could imagine happening if you took that step and did "that thing".

Prevent:
Write down the answer to: What could "I" do
to prevent these things from happening OR
decrease the likelihood of them occurring?

Repair:
If the worst-case scenario has happened, what
could "I" do to repair the damage?

Who could I ask for help? There is a question Tim asks in
his Ted Talk that I want you to ask yourself: What is the cost
of inaction?

Try this strategy out and let me know if this was helpful!

Remember: Fear is never the problem, we all fear…it's what
we do with that fear that matters.

THE IMPORTANCE OF KNOWING OUR EMOTIONS

According to psychologist and researcher David Elkind,
"…emotions are a kind of internal weather that reflects the
direction in which we feel life's currents are carrying us." In
light of this, we must know how we feel about every situation
to have a better understanding of why we react or respond
the way we do. Because, if not, chances are high that these
responses will come out negatively, triggering a downward
spiral into depression and anxiety attacks. Thus, identifying
what causes these feelings is the first step to revealing what
lies beneath them. It's also important that we understand why
people close to us behave the way they do, keeping in mind

that we cannot understand them completely. When we do not know what they are feeling, it's best to avoid projecting our emotions and expectations on them because chances are we will be disappointed when they don't meet the unrealistic standards we set for them.

The tendency of victims of trauma to label themselves as helpless victims can also be attributed to how they perceive these experiences through their mental lens, which often results in self-pity and self-blame. Thus, this is where critical thinking comes into play since it enables us "to think with understanding and imagination about what is true or real; [and] discerning or judging." Critical thinking requires identifying and challenging one's assumptions and beliefs by considering relevant information so that it would be possible to arrive at new ideas, make better decisions, or take action.

The most important thing about developing resiliency is the readiness to look at reality as it is and not an ideal version of it. This is how we set ourselves up for success. Tenacity allows us to always find the good in every situation by looking for silver linings because sometimes they're all there is left to hold on to, especially when everything else has crumbled around us. This spirit starts with believing that what happened was meant to happen.

Once we accept this truth, we can then determine the next best thing to do, freeing us from our fears and guiding us towards a healthier mindset. It also helps us understand that suffering is not only an inevitable part of life; it's often essential for growth. The less we expect things to go our way the better chance we have at overcoming any trial or tribulation because when all else fails, there's always hope to be found in knowing that the only sure weapons against wrong ideas are better ideas.

And over time, these better ideas overcome one another until they become even more compelling than what came before them and this same principle applies to developing resiliency—one small step at a time. When we know how to be more adaptable to change, we can enjoy new experiences instead of fearing them, which allows us to broaden our perspective and understanding of the world.

If these individuals cannot see your side of things or even acknowledge how their actions have affected you, this means they're refusing to understand the complexities of the situation, which often leads to them not changing. They tend to think one-sidedly and if we want accountability from these people then we should make them answer questions as well, like how it would be possible for them to honor your feelings, needs, and wants when they don't know what they are.

If we were betrayed by someone we trusted before, regardless of whether or not our trust was misplaced, we must learn how to trust again instead of simply forgetting about the past because it's the only way we can move forward and grow as human beings. On a related note, always remember that there is no such thing as "trust without risk" because that would mean that we were taking the easy way out for our own sake.

Not only does it take hard work and discipline, but it also takes time for us to gain back what we've lost since we can't walk away from betrayal and expect to be whole again overnight. When we build trust with someone, they don't just respect us—we make them feel worthy too whether or not they deserve it. And trusting them shows these individuals how far we're willing to go even when things get tough, which is another reason why trusting the right person is half the battle.

It's best to start with those who don't demand as much from us like our neighbors or family members because they're not around us all the time and we can set boundaries for them—like how much independence we allow them to have. However, if we want someone to be able to trust us, then we need to take things slowly and work our way up from there because trusting strangers is very hard.

What's important is that we don't give up on others too soon when they fail us just like when these same individuals don't give up on us when we fail them. When people earn our trust, it becomes difficult to break their hearts because they will almost always try harder than you expect. It doesn't matter whether or not people deserve second chances but what matters most is that we do because giving up on people is one of the greatest crimes in life.

As for those who are difficult to trust, it's best to use the same tactics that they're using against us—like giving them some space or withholding some attention. It might seem simple, but these techniques usually work wonders, especially when we know how to encourage people by making them feel important, which can be done if we look at them as an opportunity instead of a problem. This makes it easier for us to adapt and accept what they have to offer.

And whenever someone tries to hurt us again, anger will inevitably arise unless we choose not to let these things bother us anymore. Then again, letting go of our grudges is easier said than done unless we can free ourselves from the past by changing our mindsets— and this is what resiliency training is all about.

Completing a resiliency training program can cause us to become more positive, which will have various health benefits because positivity allows us to heal faster, in addition to making it easier for us to overcome any setbacks while also inspiring hope in others around us. Resilient people know that they need support so when things get tough, they look for people who care about them instead of trying to go it alone, especially if bad experiences from their past made them believe that nobody would be there for them when these times come.

On another note, we must understand that everybody fails sometimes because that's the only way for us to learn. We can't expect perfection from ourselves or others. My plea to you is to embrace failure, don't dislike it, embrace it. Failure provides you with the opportunity to work on yourself. Certain situations are meant to happen, it's just in the cards. When these situations happen, and they will happen, it is your job to find an empowering meaning from it. It may be painful, but you have to find a way to use it for some good.

Failure is a part of life, it'll happen; but as long as we keep persisting and trying our best, then nothing will stop us from achieving what we desire—which is why it's important for resilient individuals to always persevere even if they make mistakes because these things make life interesting and worth living. Failure can also be a great motivator, especially when we take a look back and revisit our goals and dreams and try to figure out where we went wrong.

Next, it's important to remember that failure is not the end because as long as we keep trying then there's always the possibility of succeeding the next time. It might be tempting to give up whenever we fail, but just like Rocky Balboa once said, "It's not about how hard you get hit. It's about how hard you can get hit and keep moving forward." Another thing worth mentioning is that resilient people don't make excuses whenever they fail because these things only stand in their way to success, which makes them feel miserable.

Instead, they do their best to learn from mistakes so they can correct them and do better next time.

Let me take you back to the year 1998. I spent two years at S.U.N.Y. Binghamton, and left with Over $20,000 in student loan debt, four credits and a 1.7 GPA; officially a college dropout. Failure, right? Fast forward to 15 years later, I have a master's degree. I'm an Adjunct-Instructor teaching a course on how to be successful in college. I took my failure, Faced it, Analyzed it, Innovated from it and Leapt forward from it. Trust me, I have lived the struggle and learned from it.

What is one struggle you are dealing with in your life right now that you need to Face? I want you to picture one struggle, one you are dealing with right now or one from your past and let's see what happens to your mindset when you approach your failure from a new perspective. Instead of running from it, breathe it in with me. Let's revisit our acronym with step one:

F-Face It.

Everyone fails – you and I are not alone in this. However, not everyone is brave enough to Face their failure, to admit it. Many of us hide, we camouflage, we gaslight, we deny. But not us, the warriors. We face it. We own it. We wear our failures like a badge of honor. Because failure folks is not the end of the road, it's the beginning of a new journey. Have you Faced your failure? What does that look like to you? If not, what can you do now to Face it? What would that look like? How would that feel? Own that feeling, it's okay, it won't break you. You've got this.

A-Analyze it.

Once we have faced our failures, we analyze them. We take them apart, piece by piece, moment by moment. We dissect our actions, our decisions, our thought processes. We learn. We grow. We evolve. Because failure is the greatest teacher if we are willing to learn. What has your failure taught you? What have you learned? Are you in a place now, to rise up from that failure and never revisit it or make that mistake again? How will you grow from it?

I-Innovate from it.

Every failure is an opportunity to innovate. It's a chance to try something new, something different. It's a chance to challenge the status quo, to push the boundaries, to step out of our comfort zone. We don't repeat our failures; we innovate from them. What new thing can you do? What's your challenge? What's a change you can make? How are you going to Pivot around this failure to be an even better you in the future? Heck, even right now. What can you do?

L-Leap forward.

Failure is not a reason to stop, to give up. No, it's a reason to leap forward, to strive harder, to reach further. Because failure is not falling down, it's refusing to get up. And us? We always get up. We leap forward. What is your next step? What is your next, big, gigantic, quantum leap forward? Envision yourself in the future. What does it look like with this failure way behind you in the past?

Failure, ladies and gentlemen, is not a declaration of your inability. It's a challenge, a provocation, it's life's way of telling you, "I know you can do better, so prove me right."

My friends, I invite you to see failure from this new perspective here on out. Instead of being our greatest fear, let it be our most valuable guide. Every time we fail, we are given the opportunity to start anew, to rise from the ashes, to shine brighter. Every time we fail, we grow. And every time we grow, we win.

So let's do something right now. Everyone, stand up! Stand up tall and proud. Now repeat after me, "I Fail, I Grow, I Win!" Let's say it again louder this time, "I Fail, I Grow, I Win."

No matter where you are, no matter what you do, always remember, "I Fail, I Grow, I Win."

Always remember: Breathe in failure. Exhale success.

Let failure be your oxygen.

HOW TO RECOGNIZE THE SIGNS OF TRAUMA AND A LIFE OF RESILIENCY

It is known that traumatic events in one's life can have a lasting effect on them emotionally and/or mentally.

People have different reactions to trauma; some may completely shut down after the event occurs while other people can move forward with their lives after the tragic incident has passed. There are proven techniques for overcoming what appears to be impossible obstacles after they come into your life, this includes personal tragedy or loss. These tips will help you move forward in becoming resilient no matter what blows your world apart.

The first step in overcoming trauma is to understand why it's happening. Many factors can contribute to life-altering events like this. Some of these causes include PTSD (post-traumatic stress disorder), depression, anxiety attacks, inferiority complexes, and self-esteem issues. To help with the healing process there are several steps you should take after a hard time has occurred in your life.

First of all, if possible, try to surround yourself with others who care about you. It might be easier said than done to find people who will love and accept you for who you are while going through a tough time; however, if any friendships have been severed due to a tragic experience, then focus on becoming closer with family or even pets that care about your feelings.

Surrounding yourself with people who love you unconditionally will help bring a new perspective to your life and make you realize that not everyone is going to judge or leave you even if something terrible happens.

Another important step for moving forward from traumatic experiences is self-reflection. Two techniques I suggest are writing down thoughts/feelings in a journal and creating a website where people can post their thoughts about a specific incident. This is a therapeutic way of dealing with what's going on in your mind because it allows you to think about the situation rather than just face it head-on without any guidance. With this technique, you have time to think through things before actually deciding how you feel; also, by sharing your problems with others you might find some new and helpful advice to use.

Once you have accepted and thought through everything that has happened, it is time to move forward with the help of a therapist or other professional who can guide you along the way. Self-reflection is only one side of the coin when trying to overcome traumatic experiences. A therapist/counselor will be there as a support system as well as someone else who knows how to deal with these issues once and for all.

It's important not to forget about yourself while going through this process of counseling because if you can't support yourself then no one else will be able to do it for you. Make sure you eat right, get enough sleep, exercise, and listen to music that makes you enjoy life more.

If there is anything you can take away from this book, it's that no matter what traumatic event has happened in your life, try to remember who you are inside and out because the person people love the most is you.

HOW TO REBUILD YOUR MENTAL HEALTH AND THE POWER OF RESILIENCY

Many people are unaware that they are suffering from a severe illness or disease until they physically break down at work or home where others who care for them notice their changes in physical appearance, behavior, etc. A person may look happy on the outside but on the inside they feel emotionally drained because of what is happening in their life. One way you can begin rebuilding yourself is by first writing out your feelings about what has happened to you before you let it fester so deep within your core that it becomes visible to everyone around you. The best advice any therapist can give you is to write down your feelings for at least 30 minutes a day. You can begin by writing down, whether it is everyday occurrences or events, what makes you feel happy, sad, angry, and so on.

When you begin to accept these different feelings, thoughts, and aspects, you will be able to face them head-on without feeling like you are losing something within you. This method has been highly recommended by mental health professionals because once you can block out some of the negativity surrounding you, more good things will come into your life, which will spark the element of hope within your heart.

It's release time!

When you write down your feelings, whether it's in a diary, a notebook or on a notepad, this allows them to be seen by our eyes and we can begin to process the emotions written before us. In turn, this will help break up those walls surrounding your heart so that you will have more room for good, positive emotions because once the bad ones have been taken away from you then there is more space for happiness and joy within you.

Over time, as a person who has suffered from depression begins to pick themselves back up piece by piece, they can finally see that there is a light at the end of the long dark tunnel they have been stuck in for months if not years. The hard part about going through this type of recovery period is looking back at all those memories of a person who was lost and not knowing how to reach out for help because you either fear that people will think you're weak or what others may say about your situation. The first step is to remove yourself from the toxic relationship or situation that has been going on for far too long and then you can work on rebuilding every aspect of the outside as well as the inside so that one day soon things will finally begin to look up.

Recovering from depression can be a slow process, but with the right type of support from friends, family, mental health professionals, and even spiritual therapists, there is no limit to how far you can go in recovery. It just takes a lot of time and effort along with a little bit of patience to get through this trying time in your life.

The power of developing tenaciousness in overcoming traumatic events has been well documented in research studies. It is the ability to bounce back from stressful, life-changing experiences in a positive manner that contributes to an individual's overall sense of happiness and fulfillment. This spirit is what helps build your immune system against stress.

HERE ARE SOME TIPS ON HOW TO DEVELOP A STRONG SPIRIT OF RESILIENCY:

1) Stay healthy

Your body reacts negatively when it is reacting positively towards something else. That negative reaction can be brought about by a stress response when your body believes you are under attack even if only psychologically at work. The best way to maintain or restore balance in your system is to stay healthy. Healthy eating with frequent exercise can help you have a healthier mind and body, which leads to being able to cope with stress better.

2) Manage stress

Everyone experiences stress in their lives at some point or another. Anxiety, fear, and sorrow are all normal human emotions that surface when people experience traumatic events that trigger flashbacks of previous painful experiences. Think about the worst thing that has ever happened to you and realize these feelings are not permanent but only temporary until the event passes by. Seek help from friends or family who understand what you are going through because talking about it with someone will make you feel less alone with your problems.

3) Express yourself

It is okay to express what you feel. When you start feeling overwhelmed with emotions that seem like they are out of your control, write a letter or a list of ways you can move forward. Doing things that make you happy will put you in a positive light and help balance the negative feelings inside.

4) Connect with others

As much as it may be hard for people who have experienced traumatic events before, being lonely only makes the process harder because no one can relate to what you are going through. Being alone all the time will only deepen the loneliness so reaching out to other people will give you an avenue to examine your thoughts and feelings without being judged by those who might not understand.

5) Don't blame yourself

If you experienced trauma, don't blame yourself by thinking that everything is your fault. Remind yourself that what happened was not because of anything you have done but because of the circumstances around it. A traumatic event doesn't happen just once in a lifetime so accept it as part of life. It will forever be etched in your memory, but you can choose how to make sense out of it through developing a spirit of tenaciousness.

6) Practice gratitude

Every day, take the time to write down five things you are grateful for. This simple act will help put your problems into perspective and remove negative feelings about what happened. When you appreciate and value the good things in life more than the bad, it is easier to work towards coping with a traumatic event more effectively.

7) Find purpose

Everyone needs meaning in their lives and that comes from finding something you care about or find meaningful enough for you to feel that drive to do well at it. It doesn't matter what it is as long as taking part in it makes you feel like all of your hard work has paid off in some way. The more significant the activity is the better your chance of recovering quickly from the traumatic event.

8) *Have fun*

When you are enjoying yourself, you are less likely to be stressed about matters that seem important but aren't really. Take time every day for activities that make you feel wonderful and happy, whether it is spending time with friends or taking up a new hobby. Take pleasure in the moment instead of dwelling on painful feelings from the past.

9) *Acceptance*

You can never escape your past experiences because they have become an integral part of who you are today. What matters is how much value you place on remembering what happened and how much negative emotion surrounds them because if it does not matter, then it will only hold you back from doing better things in the present. When something horrible happens to you, it is normal to feel sad from time to time, but as long as those feelings don't prevent you from living a full life, they are nothing to worry about.

10) *Take care of yourself*

The best way of dealing with a traumatic event is to take care of your body and mind. If anything makes you feel uncomfortable or unhappy, talk about it with someone who will understand what you are going through. The most important thing in developing a spirit of resiliency is the knowledge that the only person who knows how you feel inside is you, so always be true to yourself. There is a common theme one will see throughout their life after a traumatic event. Whether it's a natural disaster or just a terrible experience that may have been caused by another individual(s), the effects on an individual are everlasting throughout one's lifetime. The effects can last for days, weeks, months, and even years after the incident has happened. In some cases, the effects of the event can be so bad that people may not want to live anymore, or, worse yet, they may even attempt to take their own lives because they feel as if there is no purpose in living anymore because of what has taken place. This is why developing a spirit of spring is crucial to moving on from these types of events and continuing to live your life to the fullest.

Developing a resilient spirit can be achieved in many ways, whether it's taking the time to clear your head or talking about your experience with someone who was not there during the event itself. This is why developing a spirit of tenacity is very important to living your life after an event has affected you drastically in some way, shape or form.

People need to know that these types of events are something they will have to face throughout their life, whether directly or indirectly caused by yourself, family members, friends, work associates, etc. It does not matter what type of trauma has taken place either because it could be something as simple as losing someone close to you or something catastrophic like a natural disaster. Events such as these can and will affect people throughout their lifetime and they must learn how to develop a spirit of tenaciousness to get through these types of traumatic experiences and become successful individuals in society today.

The effects on the individual after experiencing the event are very difficult with some people having more trouble dealing with the incident itself than others depending on many factors throughout an individual's life, but there are ways in which an individual can help themselves when coping with certain situations. One way is by talking about your experience with others whether it be family members, friends, or co-workers, etc. This gives individuals who may feel alone after the event an opportunity to realize that they are not alone and it also helps them cope with what has happened. Talking about your feelings, emotions, and thought processes around the situation with someone else who was not there is one of the most effective ways in which you can begin coping with the incident itself.

Another way in which individuals typically cope with traumatic events is by writing down their thoughts and experiences throughout this time frame whether it be directly or indirectly caused by you or others. This allows you to express your true feelings towards what has happened instead of saving it all up for later when something even more severe arises. After all, they don't know how to deal with these types of situations mainly because they haven't learned how to develop the right spirit.

These two methods of coping with traumatic events are used as a way to help the individual cope and continue moving on throughout their life without letting anyone's incident affect them as much as it did before. Individuals need to understand that there will be many different types of situations in which they have to find ways of coping, but no matter what situation arises there is always a solution to help you through the tough times. Although every individual has their way of dealing with certain incidents, developing a spirit of tenaciousness is very effective for individuals to move on from certain traumatic experiences and become successful within society today.

SELF-CARE STRATEGIES FOR THOSE WITH A HISTORY OF TRAUMATIC EXPERIENCES

Many individuals have experienced traumatic events in their life, and it can be especially difficult to cope properly with these traumas. Whether the individual experienced trauma during their childhood or adulthood, having a history of traumatic experiences can greatly impact their ability to recover from stressful situations. This is because the experience of trauma often results in several long-lasting emotional effects such as fear, anxiety, anger, guilt, and sadness, thus resulting in difficulty coping with everyday life. The following are several self-care strategies that may aid those with a history of traumatic experiences by reducing feelings of stress and restoring one's healthy emotional state. However, please remember that this list does not encompass every strategy available for promoting self-care after experiencing a trauma, and it is also important to remember that these strategies may or may not work for you.

Exercise: Exercise is one of the most advantageous activities for promoting physical and emotional health (American Psychological Association 2008). Although exercise can be considered a form of stress, it often reduces feelings of depression by increasing endorphin levels in the body. A study done on women who had recently experienced traumatic events suggested that those who participated in aerobic exercises three times per week reported greater life satisfaction than those who did not participate in any type of exercise program at all.

Journaling: Journaling has become increasingly common as a way to express oneself without having anyone else read what you have written. Journaling about a traumatic experience allows the individual to work through their feelings without having them bottled up inside. This can be especially helpful if the person has trouble speaking with friends or family members about their negative experiences. If the individual does not have anyone they feel comfortable talking to, journaling can be a good way for them to express themselves and communicate their thoughts with no one but themselves.

Mindfulness: Mindfulness is an increasingly popular form of therapy that focuses on living in the present moment and maintaining nonjudgmental awareness (Rodriguez-Santos 2015). One study done on women who had experienced human sexual trafficking found that those individuals who practiced mindfulness meditation had more positive emotions than those who did not meditate.

Music: Listening to music has been shown to improve mood and reduce anxiety (American Psychological Association 2008). One study shows that when people who had experienced trauma listened to their favorite music, they were able to pay attention better than those in the control group.

Meditation: Meditation is an increasingly popular form of therapy that involves focusing on one's breathing while observing one's thoughts without judgment. The purpose is not complete thought suppression but rather learning how not to be controlled by automatic thoughts and feelings caused by a traumatic experience. Individuals who have experienced a traumatic event can use meditation as a way to calm their minds and focus on self-care without being distracted by negative emotions associated with past experiences.

Sleeping: Individuals who have experienced trauma often sleep less than those who haven't. However, lack of sleep can lead to moodiness and stress, which may prolong an already difficult experience. Getting a sufficient amount of sleep is essential for those dealing with post-traumatic stress disorder as it allows the brain to process thoughts and emotions without being distracted by feelings associated with not sleeping enough.

Socializing: Socializing after a traumatic experience is important because humans naturally function better in groups than alone. Those who have had negative experiences want others to validate their feelings and offer support during their recovery process. According to one study done on women who were sexually harassed at work, female victims who received social support from family members and friends were more likely to report their experiences than those who did not receive that type of emotional support.

Spending Time in Nature: Research shows that spending time in nature has a positive effect on one's mental health. Nature can have a calming influence on humans, leading them to feel more relaxed and self-sufficient. The natural environment reduces stress levels by increasing the strength of the parasympathetic nervous system, which regulates feelings of relaxation and calmness. Spending time in nature also gives people a chance to reflect without distractions from technology or other environmental factors that could potentially trigger negative emotions associated with past or current traumas.

Writing: Writing about one's positive thoughts and experiences has been shown to improve mood. One study found that those who wrote about traumatic events experienced better physical health outcomes than those who did not write. The researchers suggest that writing can be used as a form of stress management because it gives the individual an opportunity to challenge their thinking regarding past or current situations.

An individual may develop tenacity through experiencing several different types of stress-management techniques, such as meditation, music, spending time in nature, socializing with friends and family members, sleeping regularly, and journaling. These practices can help individuals to process emotions without feeling overwhelmed.

Some other ways to develop grit might involve building positive relationships with other people, taking care of one's physical health by eating well and exercising regularly, having a support system in place when things get difficult, and believing in oneself. For example, if one is trying to attend school or work while recovering from trauma, having supportive family members to take care of children or pets can help improve quality of life.

Believing that one will be able to cope positively with whatever life throws at them is an important part of developing tenacity. Those who feel empowered believe they can change their circumstances even though the situation may seem negative.

When it comes to mental health recovery from traumatic experiences, many individuals benefit from receiving some type of counseling. Someone who experienced traumatic events in the past may continue to feel overwhelmed by memories of those experiences if they do not resolve their emotions. Counseling can help individuals process the impact that the trauma has had on their life, find ways to work through difficult periods and develop skills for coping with future stressors.

Ways to tell if you or someone else has been traumatized:

Emotional and physical pain, withdrawing from others and avoiding relationships, difficulty sleeping and concentrating, nightmares or flashbacks, irritability and agitation, feelings of isolation and hopelessness.

According to a report from the Department of Veteran Affairs, "As many as 20 percent of Americans have been diagnosed with PTSD at some point in their lives."

As stated before, there is a chance that this could happen to you or someone around you so it would be good to know what PTSD is and how it can affect your life.

"Posttraumatic stress disorder (PTSD) is considered an anxiety disorder. It's normal for one who experiences trauma to go through numerous emotions like fear, anger, guilt, helplessness, or sadness. Those feelings may last for weeks or even months afterward."

THE SYMPTOMS OF SOMEONE WITH PTSD CAN BE:

Nightmares and flashbacks, avoidance of people, places, or things that remind them of the traumatic event, trouble sleeping and concentrating, anxiety and hypervigilance. "It is normal to experience some stress or fear when you've been through a life-threatening event such as combat but if your reaction is significantly out of proportion then it's time to seek help."

"PTSD affects 8 million adults every year. PTSD symptoms usually begin within three months after a person experienced or witnessed a traumatic event, but sometimes may not appear until years later." Many people turn to drugs such as marijuana and alcohol to try to get rid of the pain they feel on daily basis. It might sound like a good idea at the time, but doing drugs is only going to make things worse.

"People who have been through traumatic experiences tend to turn to alcohol or drug use to cope with the emotional pain they are feeling. Drugs and alcohol can help diminish emotional pain in the short term, but actually, increase long-term anxiety and depression."

TREATMENT FOR POST-TRAUMATIC STRESS DISORDER (PTSD)

This is most effective when a person's emotional response to trauma is addressed. In essence, it's all about managing the symptoms. When the symptoms aren't being managed, people with PTSD tend to have trouble functioning in their jobs, relationships, and lives.

For the treatment of PTSD symptoms to be effective, a person with PTSD needs to identify what makes them feel safe and calm. This becomes a coping strategy that can be used whenever they feel triggered by something that reminds them of their traumatic event(s). Creating a sense of safety and calm can be done through taking deep breaths or listening to music that helps reduce stress levels; whatever the individual finds soothing is then practiced as often as possible until it becomes second nature.

Another helpful tactic is practicing cognitive restructuring. This involves thinking about what triggers a person and the feelings that arise as a result and then challenging those thoughts by replacing negative self-talk with more positive thoughts. For example, instead of saying, "I am never going to be able to control my stress levels," people can say something such as, "I know I can feel calm again if I just take some deep breaths."

Post-traumatic stress disorder is treatable; however, it's important to understand the symptoms before seeking treatment. A trained mental health professional can assist with diagnosis and creating an individualized PTSD recovery plan.

CHAPTER 3

The Five M's of Success

Activating Your Operating System

Imagine your life is a powerful, state-of-the-art smartphone. It's sleek, capable, and filled with potential. But without an operating system like Android or iOS, it's just a fancy paperweight. Your life is the same—you have immense potential, but without the right operating system to guide you, you can't function at your highest level. If I may introduce you to "The Wake The Beast Way," my personal operating system is built on five pillars: Mindset, Motivation, Money, Management, and Massive Movement. Let's unlock your potential and transform your life from living in scarcity to thriving in prosperity.

Let's unpack those - and I'll share what it looked like for me as I went through that journey of going from living in scarcity to living in prosperity. I had to live the Wake the beast way and implement the 5 M' formula for success.

MINDSET

I had to transition from having a victim mindset to a creator mindset. I had to come to terms with the fact no one was coming to save me from myself. I had to settle into a life of independence, accountability and trust in self. I had to learn to turn every aspect of my life into an opportunity for learning & growth regardless of the outcome. I had to transition from having an employee mind, and even an entrepreneur mind, to having an Empire Builder mind.

I sure did say more than an entrepreneur; You see as an empire builder your success won't be defined by a specific dollar amount. Instead it will be defined by your diversified streams of income, and the reach and influence of you and your empire.

I remember when I left the military, I was in the pits; I was blaming everybody from Uncle Sam, my leadership... Everyone accept the only person responsible for my scenario at that time. ME!

There are two types of mindset: Victim & Creator. Let's examine the difference between the two.

VICTIM Mentality:

People who don't believe they're in control of their successes or failures, and often feel helpless or without blame. They are driven by pessimism, fear and anger!

VICTIMS:

- focus on their weaknesses
- make excuses
- They Compare themselves unfavorably to others
- They Predict Defeat and Give Up
- They TRY (they are ok with checking the box, "i made an attempt")
- They see problems as permanent

THE QUESTION IS: Why would anyone want to have a victim mindset?

There are BENEFITS to being a victim:

One main reason is that they have a desire to coast through life. See when you don't take responsibility for anything what happens is:

- You get a lot of attention
- Others are less likely to criticize you
- You feel you have a right to complain
- You are comfortable with blaming others
- There's always something interesting going on in your life, emphasis on interesting... translation: (some kind of drama)

It doesn't take any effort to be a loser. It doesn't take drive to be on the bottom.

QUOTE: "Ease is the greatest threat to progress than hardship"!

CREATOR MENTALITY:

On the other side of the coin you have CREATORS, they're built different :

- They Focus on how to improve
- Seek Solutions
- Turn complaints into request
- Seek help from those more skilled
- Treat problems as temporary
- Accept Responsibility
- They think positively and look for a better choice
- They DO (action driven)

I encourage you to be a creator!

▌ MOTIVATION

First I had to stop lying…. To myself mainly. I was a professional half truth teller. Two types of lies I would tell: the lies I told myself about me and the lie s I consistently told the world about me. Unless your foundation is based in the facts; no matter what you declare it'll simply be fantasy!

Self-Reflection

I was disgusted with where I was in life, living in scarcity; and had aspirations for a greater life! I grew up in poverty, a low income community, high crime, high drug use, no signs of hope. At one point or another in life we all are in circumstances or lift4^&e scenarios that aren't ideal and unfavorable. We have two choices: This is it or there is more.

This mindset has an approach where you concede to the circumstances and accept things as they are. Versus "There is more" mindset where you know deep down that abundance is waiting for you, you know that you have gifts to give the world. You know that where you are in life can't be it. The latter is where you want to be, that's where you want to draw inspiration from.

One super power we all possess but unfortunately don't activate, is "imagination"! It is free to dream good people, and it doesn't cost a thing more to dream BIG! I encourage you to look beyond where you are in life, imagine the life you want. I always say that each day is a blank canvas, paint the life you want.

Relating to motivation, here is where you ask yourself, "what is my WHY"! Its really important that you identify and write down your reasons. Whenever you embark on a journey, it is exciting in the beginning, but along the way it will get hard and you will get bored in pursuit of the objective. However, when you have a strong why, when your reasons are at the forefront of your mind it will give you the will to continue pushing forward.

▌MONEY

I know I know you on that paper chase. Well I stopped chasing money and began to chase my purpose. Remember your purpose didn't get postponed because of a pandemic. It was planted and needs to be sought after, and when found watered. It takes time, you're building a new momentum. My advice is work hard and keep improving yourself. Your gifts will make room for you, indeed! One thing I learned is that the secret to success is GIVING! A book I recommend, "The Go Giver" by Bob Burg and John David Man.

They talk about the five laws of stratospheric success and once I learned of these laws, I began to live by them.

The Law of Value

Your true worth is determined by how much more you give in value than you take in payment.

The Law of Compensation

"Your income is determined by how many people you serve and how well you serve them"

The Law of Influence

Your influence is determined by how abundantly you place other people's interest first

The Law of Authenticity

The most valuable gift you have to offer is yourself.

The Law of Receptivity

The key to effective giving is to stay open to receiving

MANAGEMENT

Here is the reality, you are the CEO of your life!

Proximity is Power

Conduct a friend and "Family" audit! Often times its the people closest to you who need to go. (Don't fight me family') You need to Identify toxic people in your life and remove them. It doesn't matter if you knew boo boo, kee kee and karen for 20 years or ya'll went to school together; if they are toxic, guess what? They gotta go!

I had to create my covert crew; This is the small group of people who you would need to go to the next level. Some people think they can do it alone. Absolutely not, you need a team.

Seal TEAM SIX

Six people I needed on my team:

- Doubter
  - The devil's advocate; asks the hard questions and sees problems before they arise; blindspots
- Instigator
  - This person pushes you –
- Example
  - Your mentor; the person you seek to emulate
- Taskmaster
  - Your accountability partner, the one who demands you get things done.

- Cheerleader
  - This person is a huge fan & strongest supporter; they love ANYTHING you do!
- Connector
  - This person gets you in places you couldn't' get into on your own; They help you find new allies!

I would identify who these people are and tell them who they are for you and that you need them. Then put them to work. Of course you need to put in the work too!

TIME

QUOTE: Time is an irreplaceable asset.

I became overprotective of my time. I also became super intentional with my time. For example:

Planning time

Every sunday I block off about an hour and map out the upcoming week and forecast the month ahead. I swear by that DND button on my phone. It allows me to focus on projects. Do I miss some important calls sometimes, sure but, I can always call them back.

Study Time

I set protected time for time to consume content. Youtube university, where I watch speeches and ted talks. Review courses, webinars and read books.

Event time

I attend networking events frequently. Here is where the magic happens. You never know who you will meet out at an event / happy hour mixer. I am in my element where I get to talk my talk. It does help that I'm a storyteller. For those who may say, "I'm an introvert, that's not my jam". Or "I don't do well in those settings"! Two books I'll recommend both by Dale Carnegier: How to win friends and influence people and how to make yourself unforgettable. You're welcome. Let me know how things go after you read those. If you are still struggling, hit me up!

MASSIVE MOVEMENT

It's one thing to have the knowledge and know what you need to do. Getting ACTIVE is where the magic happens. This very well could be the most challenging of the five M's...

As for me, I had to recover from my addiction to Mental Masturbation. That is where you have these high level conversations about ideas you have, with other smart people BUT there was absolutely no action behind it... talk talk talk! I had to reach mastery of strategic action. I stopped changing my target/goal. See when we are in pursuit of something and as we get knee deep into doing that thing we realize, sheesh this is hard. OR Sheesh this is going to take longer than I expected. Then what do we do, we change the target. Maybe we wanted to be a doctor and then we realized how hard it would be to pass the MCAT, so we decided to pursue being a Physician assistant. That is an example of scaling back or changing the target. What I learned and would suggest is this, increase your actions. If you want to be a physician, and you have a strong why dig deep and exhaust all options to assist with learning the MCAT material and go all in.

I always share with my students the concept of the Four C's:

Commence: Get started
Commit: truly lock in to whatever it is you want to accomplish.
    (Burn the boat & take the island)
Consistency: It is super important to be consistent, it will
    take time but keep at it.
Complete: Whatever you start, finish.

I stopped retreating and doing average movement to massive movement

I was setting subpar goals; I began setting crazy goals. These goals were big and I had no clue how I'd hit them. That is where the sauce lies, don't worry about the how, identify the destination/ the outcome. Things will fall into place.

I made small changes in my routine/daily habits. The book Atomic Habits by James Clear is literary gold. I read and re-read that book and adopted those atomic habits. I Incorporated the four laws of behavior change

- NOTICE IT - make it obvious
- WANT IT - Make it attractive
- DO IT - Make it easy
- LIKE IT - Make it satisfying

Remember, every smartphone needs its operating system to run efficiently and unlock its true capabilities. Similarly, embracing "The Wake The Beast Way" will help you tap into your fullest potential, transforming your mindset and life from the inside out. By mastering the five pillars— Mindset, Motivation, Money, Management, and Massive Movement—you will not only overcome obstacles but also achieve unparalleled success and fulfillment in all aspects of your life. Your journey from scarcity to prosperity is not just possible; it's inevitable when you activate your operating system. Now, let's embark on this transformative journey together and unleash the beast within.

CHAPTER 4

COME BACK FROM BROKEN

Acknowledgment and Accountability

There are going to be times in our lives when we aren't operating at our highest. We may have just experienced a setback, death, loss, heartbreak, or some other departure from what we envisioned our lives to be up until that point.

When I transitioned from the Army, I went from Staff Sergeant promotable Murphy to unemployed Shaun. For the first time in my adult life, I didn't know where the next check or meal was coming from. I was both stuck in place and on a treadmill going nowhere fast. I went from essential personnel in mission critical operations to a broken Veteran. No job, no vision, no goals, nothing!

After I got out of the military in 2006 I spent over 8 years floating.

For some time after separation I had a victim mindset. I was blaming Uncle Sam (the military), my previous leadership...

I didn't own the fact I made the decision to get out.

I didn't own the fact I didn't take it seriously when I was supposed to attend those transition classes to get prepared. Essentially, I lacked extreme ownership!

First, it is important to acknowledge that we are 100% responsible for our experiences and then we have to hold ourselves accountable for the experiences we allow into our awareness moving forward. Acknowledgment and accountability—these two things are the easiest to say and the most difficult to put into practice. So how do we go about taking these steps?

■ WHAT'S YOUR STORY?

When you feel like you are in the pit of despair after experiencing a loss, disappointment, or heartbreak (you get the picture), it can be easy to make up stories for why this is happening. The reality may be that it just happened, but this doesn't mean that's all there is to it. There are infinite possibilities out there so why not choose one that has you coming back stronger than ever before? I know what some of you may be thinking... This sounds very metaphysical/ new age-y/ woo-woo /hokey. It might feel that way, but the reality is that it works! Many of these stories are rooted in metaphysical truths and I can't argue with the results. Many times, the problem isn't even a story; it's no story at all. So instead of creating a story, just start by paying attention to what your life feels like when you aren't making up a story about why things happen or you're not acknowledging/accounting for what has occurred.

■ TIP: ACCOUNTABILITY

Take responsibility for your experiences. Don't waste your time feeling powerless to the world around you. Take full advantage of this moment; stop creating false stories in your head and slow down just enough to notice when life is telling you, "I love you so much I want more than anything to give you what you need in each moment but your resistance or lack of presence is blocking me from doing my job!"

If accountability is something new to you, please make an appointment with yourself right now—seriously do it, write it in your calendar if necessary—and make time for this every day until you are comfortable with the practice. Accountability is one of the most effective strategies for behavioral change and an integral part of tenacity. The best way to build accountability into your life is to ask for help. This may sound counterintuitive because if you are on your own why would it be necessary to ask for help? The easy answer is, well, it just takes two people to tango. Anyone can walk around feeling stuck, but it takes more courage to come out of the dark and ask for what you need. Get some accountability in action by telling someone about your personal experience with grit or how this tip spoke to you and ask them if they will hold you accountable (in a loving way of course).

■ TIP: ACKNOWLEDGMENT

Acknowledgment is as simple as taking a moment to say out loud, "I acknowledge what I'm feeling... I acknowledge what happened..." That's it! Once you do this, you can continue with your day and allow yourself the space and time to make up a story or not.

■ THE POWER OF ACKNOWLEDGMENT

Acknowledgment can be one of the most profound experiences you will ever have. It requires a very simple action—to stop, look at what is going on inside you, and acknowledge it. The more we do this practice the more we find ourselves released out of a dark cloud of pain and into a world full of love (reality). We create our reality, but our subjective experience will only change if we make it happen. Bouncy individuals can meet their needs even in difficult circumstances.

This means that no matter how much resistance or darkness you encounter along your path remember there is light waiting for you. You just have to remember that you are the one who can walk into it. I know this is easier said than done and as a self-proclaimed overthinker sometimes the darkness seems so dark and hopeless, but there is always some truth shining through if you look hard enough. After all, we don't see with our eyes, we see with our mind, so whatever you choose to believe or not believe is what your experience will be.

▮ TIP: SELF-CARE

Self-care is not just the ability to say no but refusing to accept things that are dangerous or harmful to you. For example, "I would like another helping of dessert, but I am determined not to eat it because my doctor has advised me against it." Or, "Your criticism makes me angry and causes me pain; I won't be using it anymore." It's saying yes when something nourishes you. Tenaciousness requires us to know what feeds our souls and take time out regularly for necessary renewal; this means taking care of our bodies, minds, spirits, and hearts through rest, recreation, relaxation—and yes, even play and fun!

If you feel like you need to take a self-care course this may be a sign that your grit muscles are not strong enough yet to give you what you need. This is normal and the only way to get back on track with feeling good in yourself (and your life) is by giving it time. For many of us, the process of facing our inner demons and working through them can be particularly challenging, especially if we haven't done any work on ourselves yet. It's hard to go from living unconsciously/ in reaction mode all the time to becoming conscious and choosing how we want our lives (and our days) to look every single day. If this seems too difficult for now, come back to this article after you have had some time.

TIP: CREATE AN INNER CIRCLE OF SUPPORTERS

This is the time in your life when you must nurture all of your relationships, including those not related to work. And don't limit this group just to family and friends; consider people who can provide you with encouragement or advice, including good books that can help you. Nurture each relationship through quality time, phone calls, cards, letters, emails, texts—whatever works best for you! Don't wait until things are falling apart before you seek out support from others; that's like letting the weeds take over your perfectly planned garden because you just don't have time to weed it!

The power of tenaciousness is in creating quality relationships that support you when the going gets tough. Stepping it up a notch, consider asking your close friends and family what they think might be important for you to do to cultivate this powerful practice in your life—not only will they appreciate the chance to give their input but this could become an interesting "exercise" (if you can call it that) for them too!

Our social connections provide us with information about the world around us; people who are experiencing or witnessing similar things to us can help us through tough times because we feel less alone. This could be anything from advising on how to deal with an unsupportive spouse to suggestions of where to apply for jobs. The more time you spend with people who care the more opportunities you'll have to uncover solutions that will help you reach your goals.

CHAPTER 5

BUILD YOURSELF

Create a healthy self-concept

There is a polar response to everything in the universe. For up there's down, for right there's left, and so on. Reframe negative thinking and habits. If up until now you've chosen cigarette smoking to manage your stress, switch that to five minutes of deep breathing. If you've chosen alcohol to numb negative emotions, opt for running or exercise. By consistently reframing the negatives we strengthen our ability to create good habits that yield the results we desire.

Self-talk is important. Think about what you are saying to yourself in your head. Is it positive? Is there encouragement, love, and positivity? Or is it negative messages that you give yourself over and over throughout the day?

As an example:

"I'm so stupid! I can't believe I made this mistake again! Everyone will think I'm dumb! What do I have to do around here to get noticed? This job sucks! And so does my life!"

The above messages are very destructive, not only for oneself but also for anyone who has to listen to them being said aloud.

Embrace mistakes—they teach us a valuable lesson. They show us what we need to change so they aren't repeated again and again. If a person makes three mistakes a day, it's not about getting rid of the mistake but rather it is taking the time to learn the lessons that come with making these mistakes. Mistakes can be looked at in an entirely different light when you reframe them in your mind... *I made another mistake today... Okay, well, this is what I need to look out for next time so I don't repeat this action!*

The point here is that perfectionists or high achievers tend to take everything personally. Therefore, everything becomes much more important to them. They are much harder on themselves than they would ever be on anyone else. And that's not healthy!

By being too hard on yourself it sets up a negative self-concept. If you are always faulting yourself for things you can't control, then eventually this will slip into other areas of your life as well where the same thing happens over and over again because you created an identity about yourself that is filled with negativity. Whether it be calling yourself names or thinking harshly all the time, this will become part of who you believe yourself to be ... and before long, these thoughts leak over into other aspects of your life until at some point there is nothing but despair left in your life.

And that's not what you want! You can take control of this. It starts with your thoughts and beliefs about yourself. Be gentle; be loving; be compassionate towards yourself when others would not likely be so generous towards you when you make mistakes or fail at something.

When things go wrong in our lives, sometimes it is too easy to rehash these events over and over in your head... *If only I had done this instead of this ... then everything would be okay now... If only I was better looking/smarter/completely different than who I am now...* Then people would like me more... This constant reflection on past events is very damaging because the person fixates on what they believe are their "faults" and attributes these as character flaws. This person has developed a negative self-concept because they believe everything they don't like about themselves cannot be changed.

And you can change it! We all can, together ... because even though we are all different people, the amazing thing about our universe is that what affects one of us affects everyone else on this planet in some way or another. We are collectively linked, positively or negatively.

If you find yourself stuck in pain physically or emotionally, look outwards instead of inwards. Instead of dwelling on how badly your body feels, focus on outside things—whether it be (1) engaging in conversation with someone, (2) finding a new perspective on your situation by looking at it from another person's perspective, or (3) trying to find some humor in the situation.

This is what grit training is all about and although it can be hard (believe me I know), this kind of training is something we must all learn to do if we want to make positive changes in our lives and especially in these difficult times we live in.

As my dear friend says, "No matter what happens around you, always try to keep smiling!"

IDENTIFY YOUR STRENGTHS AND WEAKNESSES

Chances are you're not good at everything. Perhaps an assignment has come up that is outside your skillset. Recognizing what you're bad at and knowing where to best spend your time for optimal results will keep you from wasting energy on things you won't be successful at.

It's human nature to focus on what we perceive is wrong in our lives, the negative things that happen to us or around us, but it is also important to recognize our strengths and weaknesses because this knowledge helps develop an accurate self-concept. When we have an accurate self-concept, we can focus on those things that we excel at and capitalize on our strengths. We also recognize the areas where we need to improve and then work towards not just improving but truly mastering those skills that come more naturally for us. Even if you have a strong desire to improve certain areas of your life but you recognize that they aren't strengths of yours, it is okay! Everyone has unique talents and abilities. If something isn't one of yours, there are other things about you that you can use to define who you truly are.

Some people struggle with having negative thoughts or low self-esteem. This negatively impacts the way they interact with others. Individuals like this often don't work well in groups because they may feel uncomfortable talking to others, inferior to them, unworthy of receiving respect from others, etc. These feelings can be positive or negative depending on how you perceive them. If every thought is interpreted as an attack on your self-worth, it can be difficult to have a healthy perspective on things.

This is why it's important to recognize your strengths and weaknesses so you know the best way to optimize your time spent learning new skills or improving on old ones without overloading yourself with too much information. If you are not great at something, that's okay! Just spend more of your time on those areas where you excel before trying to learn new subjects. Being comfortable talking in front of people may be difficult for you if you are shy, but not everyone needs to be an expert public speaker for their career goal. Maybe one day you will develop enough confidence in this area, but there are other ways to express yourself instead of speaking extemporaneously in front of a group, so try to focus on your strengths.

KNOW WHEN YOU ARE MAKING PROGRESS

A great way to maintain positive momentum is by knowing when real progress has been made. This can be done simply by keeping track of what you've done during the day or week. If you have a long list, it may feel overwhelming, but break it down into smaller chunks that are easier to manage. For instance, if your goal for the day is to finish an assignment that is due at midnight, try not to worry about the other things that need doing because they will still be there tomorrow! Instead, focus all your energy on completing this one task at hand before worrying about anything else. It's okay if you don't get to everything else! The things that are on the list but were not completed still matter.

If you're feeling positive about something, record it! If you do this regularly, it becomes more of a habit and you start to build up an accurate self-concept. You will begin to realize just how capable you are! This also builds confidence in your abilities.

Make sure there is no room for gray areas. If a task isn't done correctly or completely, don't let this discourage you from doing your best next time. Take note of what went wrong and come up with a plan for fixing it so that the same problem doesn't crop up again. Understanding where mistakes came from will help you avoid making them over and over again.

We are all trying to achieve our best selves. This is not an easy task if each step forward seems more like two steps back because it's easy to lose faith in yourself when you fall short of your expectations. If bettering yourself is difficult for you, start small by getting involved with things that interest you. The more passionate you are about something the easier it will be to stay focused on reaching your goals! Don't feel pressured into doing things that make you uncomfortable at first; it takes time to ease into a new situation.

But if you focus on pushing your comfort zone and trying new things, eventually those 'bad' experiences will start to become some of the best memories from your life!

The power of developing the spirit can change your life. Whenever something good happens, take some time to appreciate it and let the people around you know how much their support means to you! These small changes have a positive cumulative effect that keeps re-energizing you as opposed to draining away your willpower until there is nothing left. Maintaining a positive attitude does not mean there won't be any bumps along the road, but if you go into each day with determination and purpose it leads to overall happiness.

TAKE RESPONSIBILITY FOR YOUR CHOICES AND ACTIONS

We all answer for our choices and actions, whether people hold us accountable or not. People who stand by idly as others make bad decisions are enablers; they support the wrongdoing of another person because they're afraid of confronting them about their errors. Enablers may think they're helpful, but in reality enabling any alcoholic to drink is only going to prolong their getting better. It's important to know when to take responsibility and do not allow yourself to be manipulated by others because of an unwillingness to confront them about their bad choices, especially if it is dangerous or potentially damaging to themselves or others.

You have the ability to choose your reactions and develop a positive attitude. No matter what happens, there's always going to be a choice in how you perceive it. You can stay upset about something for a long time or allow yourself to let it go and move on with your life.

There are so many factors that influence our lives from childhood up to adulthood, but we have control over ourselves and only ourselves. We have the power to change our mentality and become better people with the help of others who share similar goals! Don't let past mistakes hold you back from achieving self-growth!

It doesn't matter if everyone else thinks something is impossible; if you want to achieve something and you believe in yourself, you can do it! Push your boundaries and put forth the effort into achieving the best self that you possibly can. You might end up surpassing your expectations!

As children, we get many messages from adults about what we should be capable of doing, like tying our shoes or making a PB&J sandwich on our own. Sometimes these messages stick with us but other times they don't. No matter how old we are there is always room for growth and improvement; it's never too late to take a step back and re-evaluate where we stand in terms of where we want to go.

The most important person in charge of getting better is always you.

DON'T LET YOUR FEELINGS RULE YOU

It can be hard sometimes if a person has a low sense of self-esteem, but the way you feel does not have control over you. Sometimes we believe what other people say about us and this creates really low levels of self-worth. We judge our actions harshly while giving other people a free pass for their poor behavior. The hardest thing that can happen in life is losing hope and confidence in your abilities, thus becoming dissatisfied with who you are.

People are not always going to agree with the choices you make, nor should they. Allowing other people's opinions to affect your behavior is a recipe for disaster because it means that their emotions are dictating yours. If someone doesn't like what you do, they can choose to express themselves about it, but until then you have complete control over how you react to them!

Letting your feelings rule your actions is a major problem in relationships. We all get angry sometimes, but when we hold on to our anger too long, it often brings out the worst in us when we finally let loose on another person with cruel words or actions. People who are being abusive will never change if they know that, when push comes to shove, you'll always be the one who apologizes first.

PRACTICE BEING ASSERTIVE WITHOUT BEING AGGRESSIVE.

An assertive person is someone who can confidently express their opinions and emotions in a way that doesn't escalate into hostility or fear. It takes practice to develop your assertiveness levels, but it's important for healthy self-expression within relationships with others, especially those closest to us.

Being passive is also problematic because it enables bad behavior from other people who are not aware of their actions so they continue without considering how the people around them feel about what they are doing. Being passive creates an environment where there are no limits or consequences for an abuser so they continue acting badly because there are no negative consequences. If you want people to treat you better, take charge and be assertive instead of just passively enduring their actions.

An important step in self-growth is recognizing when we are being too passive or aggressive and we should change our behavior accordingly.

Once we start practicing these concepts in our relationships with others, we begin to practice them on a larger scale: how we behave toward ourselves and how we view our place in the world at large.

If you start feeling sorry for yourself, realize that this is not going to get you anywhere because it's only going to make you feel more miserable about your situation! Sometimes too much sympathy can lead us into a mental trap where everything becomes hopeless because there's no way out.

Even though life can get hard at times there are always opportunities to make things better for you. Letting your feelings rule you instead of the other way around will make you feel empowered and like you're in control of your own life!

FORGIVENESS AND GRATITUDE

By holding on to negative feelings, we not only hold on to the emotions associated with them, but we also keep ourselves in a mental state that is less than ideal for making good decisions and improving life circumstances. Forgiving and forgetting past disputes restores your sense of self-confidence and inner peace, allowing you to move forward. Letting go of the need for revenge or retribution is healthy for us, however difficult it may seem at times. When we choose to live in a space of forgiveness rather than unforgiveness, we not only free ourselves from negative emotions but also create energy around us that attracts positive things into our lives. We become more accepting of others when we are forgiving them because we're less likely to be cynical about their motives and behaviors.

Gratitude – gratitude is powerful because it takes your focus off of what you don't have and puts it on the good things in life, good things that we often take for granted. Keeping a journal of gratitude will help remind us to appreciate those things we previously took for granted and allow our minds to shift into a more positive space. Try this for a few minutes each day or even all day to give yourself a mental boost!

As you develop your spirit of grit, you'll discover that there are many opportunities in life to grow and expand. Developing a strong sense of personal responsibility will allow you to do what's best for you because it will make you feel satisfied with the decisions you make. When we understand our sense of purpose in the world, we know where we want to go and how much work it takes. It also helps us see when someone else is trying to take advantage of us so we can avoid being taken advantage of by other people. Having a clear direction in life gives us much more self-confidence than when we feel lost and unclear about our future.

In life you have two types of people: Wandering generality and a meaningful specific.

Wandering generality

- someone who has no goals and uses their time for nothing specific, they often confuse being busy with taking care of business.
- Someone going through life aimlessly, lacking clarity, consistency, and direction.

Meaningful specific

- Someone who knows what their specific purpose or meaning in life is.
- Possesses the passion and power to live their best life.

Being clear of purpose also makes it easier to achieve our goals so we can feel more satisfied with the life we are living. Having a sense of accomplishment is an important part of tenaciousness because it leads to feelings of happiness. Overall, developing a spirit of tenacity creates lifelong changes around you, your relationships, and how you approach challenges in general.

In working toward being resilient, you'll not only create strength for yourself but you will find many opportunities opening up all around you!

ADOPT A POSITIVE ATTITUDE WITH YOUR LIFE

What you think, feel, and do affects how you live. You can be effective by embracing positivity in all aspects of your life: work, family relationships, friendships, etc. By making high-quality connections with people through positivity you can boost yourself up when times get tough. Having positive thoughts allows better mental health, which leads to physical wellbeing, thus leaving room for personal growth and development—so keep stress at bay!

To be positive, you have to tell yourself that there is a solution to every problem. When you catch yourself thinking negatively, challenge these thoughts and find more positive ways of seeing things. Oftentimes we let the doubt monster take charge and it brings about "A.N.T.s", automatic negative thoughts. Remember the power lies in between your ears. It's all in your head! Having a positive attitude can make a big difference in how you feel about yourself and it also allows you to appreciate the good things in life while not taking them for granted!

For example: If your goal is to get an A on an upcoming test, going into the test with a negative mindset will only add stress and anxiety, which leads to poor focus on the task at hand, sabotaging your chances of getting that A. In this case, having a positive mindset would be that if I study hard then I have done my best work so if I do get a B on the test, it's still a great grade and I can learn from this experience instead of just giving up.

You need to invest in yourself first before anyone else! You have to be willing to take care of your own needs before anything else because if you don't your wellbeing won't matter anymore. Just like when you are on an airplane, if the oxygen mask drops you are instructed to put on your mask first. The same practice applies to your life, take care of yourself first. You are no good to anyone else if you aren't doing well. If you feel good, then everything will flow from there! The following are ways to make sure that you practice self-care:

- Getting enough sleep
- Making time for personal interests
- Listening to music or meditating

Keep your energy high by avoiding negative people and toxic environments. Negative people include those who gossip too much, creating unnecessary drama, those who complain too much, those who gossip about you to others, and those who are critical of everything. Toxic environments include workplaces that don't appreciate their employees or encourage growth, unhealthy relationships with partners and family members as well as environments such as bars where drunken people share toxic thoughts!

If someone is a negative person this is a reflection of them rather than you. Negativity can be a way for someone else to feel better about themselves, but if the energy around you feels too toxic then do what you need to do to take care of yourself!

The following strategies allow an individual to develop resiliency:

- Having good coping skills
- Exercising regularly
- Maintaining connections with others
- Maintaining a positive outlook on life

For example: When you are feeling down about yourself, find ways to get out of this mindset by reaching out to other people. If you are consistent with these strategies then your tenacity will grow stronger every day!

A goal that many people have is to become more resilient. Sometimes it can be hard for people to recognize that they are resilient already, while others don't know how to develop their grit. Resiliency is the trait of bouncing back quickly from difficulties and challenges in life because having this mindset improves your coping skills so when something bad happens you can recover faster! This also provides hope for better things happening in the future because if you think you are not capable of getting through something, then you are less likely to try.

Finding your inner strength also means knowing yourself more deeply! If you understand what triggers your stress or if certain feelings make it hard for you to be resilient the better you will be able to cope with these challenges when they arise. This is true for everyone because every individual has a unique path in life that makes them who they are. You have to learn how to accept this about you and embrace it rather than hide it away!

The best way to deal with challenging events is by anticipating them so that problems can be resolved before anything bad happens. For example: If someone knows that they fear flying, whenever they are faced with it they will start to feel nervous. If they anticipate the fear of flying before boarding a plane, their anxiety levels will be lower because they are mentally prepared for what is ahead.

Tenaciousness also helps people see the good in everything! If something bad happens, find out why it has happened so that you can learn from this experience and bounce back stronger than before! Finding new ways to help yourself deal with challenges means that you have taken your problem-solving skills to the next level, which will provide more long-term benefits for your life. This also decreases stress levels because instead of worrying about future problems it allows people to focus on the present moment rather than living in fear of what could come next.

BALANCE YOUR THOUGHTS – BALANCE YOUR EMOTIONS

It is both healthy and empowering to be balanced in our thought processes. Strive for the state of thinking positively some of the time while recognizing that negative feelings are part of everyone's life experience. Negative feelings are never something that should be permanently attached to a person's behavior or personality. We all have bad days, but don't let those days define you as a human being. Remember that just because you feel bad it doesn't mean your life is bad.

Balance out your negative thoughts with positive emotions and goals. If you find yourself ruminating on the past, try to shift towards a more hopeful future and remember all of the things in your life for which you are grateful. Also, make sure to remind yourself of what you have accomplished and how far you've come! Label these positive feelings as "emotional evidence" of good things happening to good people like you.

Developing grit can be accomplished by setting realistic goals for ourselves and basing our happiness on our emotional progress rather than materialistic achievements or wealth. Just because we lack something does not mean we are lacking anything at all.

If you think that something bad may be on the horizon it is important to anticipate how much stress this will create for you versus what you can handle currently in your life. When working through problems, putting them into perspective rather than getting overwhelmed by them is key to tenaciousness. Resolving problems as quickly as possible instead of dragging out issues allows people to push through difficult times because they are reminded that their problem doesn't define who they are! Having these positive coping skills also allows people to be more productive when facing challenges outside of their control. For example, a student who fails a test but knows how to cope with the situation by putting his/her emotions aside and looks at the situation objectively can learn from their mistakes and be better prepared to take the test again.

Finding ways to maintain positivity helps us increase our tenacity levels because being optimistic about life means that we are more likely to do something positive in our lives (such as take care of ourselves or someone else) versus focusing on the negative, which will not help you accomplish your goals. The ultimate goal is to focus on feeling good about yourself, which provides a sense of purpose, making it easier for people to see themselves in a positive light!

If something bad has happened (i.e. loss of job) then ask yourself, "What other opportunities can I take advantage of?" The world is constantly changing so why shouldn't we change with it? Some people fail to realize that things happen for a reason and, as the saying goes, what doesn't kill you makes you stronger.

For example: If you got fired from your job then use this as an opportunity to find something new rather than just sitting at home moping about the situation. There is almost always room for improvement, so don't let yourself get stuck in one place too long! This doesn't mean that if everything was horrible all of the time people would be resilient; however, if these emotions are short-lived, they won't cause many negative consequences in your life.

Living in a state of constant optimism and positivity takes hard work but it is certainly possible, especially when you have support from family, friends, or even just yourself.

Living this way may feel unnatural at first; however, after a while it will begin to feel more comfortable—much like riding a bike! Remember that everyone has bad days so just because you aren't feeling great doesn't mean anything about who you are as a person! This is all based on the idea behind emotional evidence: You can still feel good about yourself despite being upset or depressed because being human means experiencing a range of different emotions throughout your life! Just remember every emotion passes so don't focus too heavily on one feeling or another!

A good way to develop tenacity skills is to break down goals into smaller steps so that they feel more manageable. Remembering your progress along the way is a great reminder of how far you have come and this will keep you motivated and working hard on your dreams. Bouncy people use their past experiences as motivation for future endeavors, which allows them to grow and become better versions of themselves each day.

Tenaciousness can be developed through studying behavior, learning from mistakes we've made in the past, recognizing the positive aspects of our lives, identifying our core values, feeling empathy towards other people who are struggling with things that are difficult for us, etc. The key aspect behind all resilient behaviors is that there are many different ways to get the same result!

An individual's core values are their compass in life, without them they wouldn't know how to make decisions based on what is important to them. They keep people grounded so that they can stay focused rather than getting distracted by everything else going on around them. Developing strong core values helps you figure out your identity because it gives you a sense of purpose and allows you to truly feel like yourself! Respect for others, hard work, diversity—these are all aspects that should be included in strengthening one's core values. Of course, everyone has their differences, but there are many universal values that we should all aspire towards such as honesty, respectfulness, justice, etc.

Without empathy, it is difficult to develop tenacity because compassion is linked with empathy! Grit is the ability to bounce back from hard times so without empathy one might not feel bad for other people who are experiencing similar hardships.

ADOPT GROWTH THINKING – PRIORITIZE PERSONAL DEVELOPMENT

Embrace probability theory by striving for continuous improvement instead of absolute perfection. If you examine growth strategies consistently, all areas can improve with time; small steps at a time will lead to massive success over the long term. Recognizing your improvement is an excellent way to challenge yourself to take on new challenges!

People are more likely to be resilient when they have a growth mindset rather than a fixed one. A person with a fixed mindset will believe that abilities are set in stone so there is no point in trying something if you already know you won't be good at it. Someone with a growth mindset, however, believes that possibilities are endless and instead of being intimidated by obstacles, they see them as opportunities for self-improvement.

Focus on what you can control while neglecting what you cannot avoid. If you spend your whole life worrying about things out of your control then nothing will get done! Worrying translates to praying for what you don't want. You might not have any type of control over some situations, but it's still important to stay positive and try your best.

In conclusion, having a tenacious mindset is all about being flexible! You should be prepared for anything because even if you expect good things, something might happen that will make you have to re-evaluate your options. Despite any challenges that come your way, always remember that you are the only one who has the power to determine how successful or unsuccessful you will end up being!

CHAPTER 6

NQTD- NEVER QUESTION THE DECISION, COMMIT

Commitment is the fodder of champions. When we commit to ourselves and our goals NO MATTER

WHAT, we give clear instruction to the universal energy that surrounds us of our desires. From the energetic space of commitment, all the forces of the universe begin to work in tandem with our physical being to make magical things happen that transcend our current circumstances.

When we commit to ourselves and our goals NO MATTER WHAT, we give clear instructions for what we want AND ALSO the instructions of all the forces of negative energies that surround us. From this energetic space, not only do we receive magical things, but I believe these additional unseen phenomena are due to the amount of power present in such commitment.

Whether you call it God, Universe, Higher Self, Angels, or Energies, when we make a commitment, it gets registered and the sign of such registration is synchronicities!

Coincidences that go against probability happen often around those who have made a solid commitment.

People will say, "It's just a coincidence," because they cannot explain why something happened the way it did.

What you are seeing is the manifestation of your spirit of commitment. You cannot see it BUT IT IS THERE!

Awareness is how we expand our capabilities so that we can more effectively transmit these commanding forces through our words, thoughts, feelings, and actions.

Knowledge without awareness is like power without a switch; an unseen force that has no direction or control over itself. It's only by becoming aware of your own energetic space that you can begin to hone in on this energy source within you (and others if they allow it) and use it as a tool for actualizing your dreams/goals/ desires!

CHAPTER 7

DISRUPT THE MALADAPTIVE PATTERN – CONSCIOUS AWARENESS

The average human has over 70,000 thoughts a day. Think of that number in terms of eating. If we consumed 70,000 calories daily without physical activity, we would all be just as wide as we are tall. Or on the flip side of consuming that many calories in a day, we would have to maintain the same level of physical activity as an Olympic athlete to stay in top form. We must consistently observe, monitor, and reframe our thoughts during every waking hour until it becomes second nature.

DISRUPT THE MALADAPTIVE PATTERN – PHYSICAL ACTIVITY

The second half of the equation is to develop systems of positive reinforcement. This can be as simple as rewarding yourself with a few minutes per day doing something you like after completing some tasks that were deemed unpleasant (i.e., exercise, run errands, prepare for the next day). Or it could involve taking time at least once per week to spend with family or friends in an environment that fosters conversation and connection.

ESTABLISH A ROUTINE – CONSCIOUS AWARENESS

Simple steps toward establishing routines are crucial because most people who have mood disorders lack structure and/ or guidance. By default, most humans seek routine; this is typically attributed to our work patterns but can also be found at home due to family habits. We begin to seek routine in our social lives as well. For example, social media sites have become a worldwide phenomenon with the common denominator being users need guidance on how to spend time on that platform. The more structure you can incorporate into your day-to-day activities the better chance you have at disrupting an unhealthy pattern of thoughts or behaviors.

ESTABLISH A ROUTINE – PHYSICAL ACTIVITY

Routine is important because it reduces decision fatigue, which allows for quicker reaction times when encountered with unexpected circumstances outside of your control (i.e. road construction). There are only so many decisions we can make per day before our brain becomes fatigued. By having set patterns at play throughout your day, you reduce the number of decisions that need to be made.

ESTABLISH A SUPPORT SYSTEM – CONSCIOUS AWARENESS

In case you have a diagnosed mood disorder, you should already have a support system in place. But it is important to be mindful of your support network and ensure they are healthy role models for coping with stressors or supporting one another when necessary. If you find yourself unable to establish or maintain a support network, this could be an indicator of a larger problem. A general rule of thumb is to surround yourself with people who display traits that align with having healthy relationships (trustworthiness, loyalty, empathy). On the other end of the spectrum, if your circle of closest friends lacks any balance between positives and negatives then it should give you cause for concern. You do not need friends who are going to enable your maladaptive behaviors, nor do you require a group of people with whom you can only commiserate. Having balance in friendships throughout your life ensures that you have a well-rounded environment from which to draw during times of struggle.

ESTABLISH A SUPPORT SYSTEM –
PHYSICAL ACTIVITY

By building a solid foundation for yourself by intentionally choosing supportive relationships, you will strengthen the tenacity muscles that come into play when faced with unfavorable circumstances. Support systems also provide accountability and safe places where it is okay to be vulnerable or mindful of one's self. By creating this type of atmosphere in real life, we begin to build our internal resources so they become active when most (i.e. alcohol) would otherwise be passive.

CHAPTER 8

CARVE THE NEW YOU FROM STONE

An artist sets out with first the seed of creativity in his heart and then a vision. From there a piece of stone is carved out to become a beautiful work of art. This is your journey and you are the masterful artist carving yourself out of stone daily. You are the stone and you will become the masterpiece. This is your journey to self-mastery and it takes time, patience, and dedication. This is merely the beginning of the most important piece in your life—yourself. This journey will be with you for the rest of your life.

The most critical part of this process is to realize that there are two sides to every story, not just one. You must look at both sides or these truths may cause you more harm than good. For example, when you start winding down on a day and realize it's time for bed; some would say they are tired due to lack of sleep, while others would feel ecstatic because they "get" an extra hour in their day (translated: by sleeping less they get to do more). It comes down to perspective and how much energy you want to spend stressing over what people might think because you sleep less/more than them.

Instead, start focusing on understanding that there is no such thing as a bad decision. Feel the pain and struggles because this will help you appreciate the comfort and ease of things to come. Translated: if you never struggle with what to do or where to go, you'll always take the easy way out instead of standing your ground and doing what's best for you (your inner voice). The more challenging decisions that are met head-on the easier life becomes as far as taking the less challenging path.

This is why it takes time, patience, and dedication— self-mastery is not easy but it's an amazing journey! It only hurts before it starts feeling good again and you'll be stronger and better than before.

Daily, view the world as a reflection of yourself. This will help you take responsibility for your actions and how those around you react to them. Interpret everything that happens as an opportunity for growth and, as a result, don't blame other people because they're not at fault—it's just another opportunity to learn something about yourself! Take this method of thinking and apply it to every area of your life.

Diet/Fitness: The foods we eat reflect our inner health so instead of blaming "bad" food choices on anyone else, step back and appreciate the lesson behind why certain foods are making us feel bad. Then take accountability by changing what we choose to put into our bodies. You take control of what you put in, so don't point fingers at anyone else when the only person responsible for your food choices is you.

Friendships/Relationships: If someone around us is creating more negativity than positivity, it's better to look within and see why we're surrounding ourselves with this type of energy. Take accountability by removing that person from your life or changing the nature of how you interact with them (if possible). It's time to focus on building relationships that improve our lives instead of worsening them.

Happiness/Success: Stop giving away your power! When something bad happens, do you automatically assume the outcome will be negative because "things like this always happen to me"? So often people fall into this pattern where they attract negativity because they subconsciously give away their power. Learn to take these experiences and turn them into something positive. This is how you grow!

Be grateful every day for the traumatic events that happen in your life; realize that everything happens for a reason, even if at the time it doesn't make sense.

Certain situations are meant to happen. We are tasked with having to find an empowering meaning from these situations, even if it's painful, and then find a way to use it for some good. These traumatic experiences are indeed trails that are blessings in disguise if we allow ourselves to see the good in all things! By focusing on what's going right we can learn from what's going wrong, so stop seeing yourself as a victim and shift your perception by taking control of your reality.

A great way to take responsibility is to start being kinder to yourself when negative events occur instead of shaming yourself into misery. When these situations arise, ask, "What is it trying to teach me?" and instead of thinking you "deserve" bad things because of anything in your past, take a step back and appreciate the lesson attached.

If we make mistakes we should immediately move on and focus our energy on how we can be better next time! If we continue wallowing in self-pity then nothing will ever change. It's easy to beat yourself up over what happened, but the only person who benefits from this behavior is your ego because it feels nice when someone takes accountability for their actions; you're letting other people have control over your life if they know you'll always feel sorry for them. The moment you stop feeling sorry for others they no longer have power or control over you!

IDENTIFY WHAT YOU WANT TO CHANGE ABOUT YOURSELF

-You should always be willing to grow. If you're not willing to change then it's unlikely that your life will improve.

"Nothing changes if nothing changes!" The first thing that needs to happen to facilitate change is to begin the new habit-forming process. It is said to take a minimum of 21 days to form a new habit. You have successfully formed a new habit when a new behavior feels automatic. A habit feels automatic when it's a simple behavior; it feels effortless. I'm a huge fan of James Clear and his approaches laid out in his book, "Atomic Habits".

-Start by first identifying what you want to change about yourself.

If there are any issues or behaviors that stand out as ones you'd like to modify, make a daily commitment to stop this behavior for 66 days. As bizarre as it sounds, this is the exact amount of time the mind requires to create a new habit.

So, if there's anything you need to work on, such as using profanity, try to avoid using these words for three weeks and see how much more positive this makes you feel. You'll quickly realize how many people react differently towards you when you kick these bad habits.

If there are certain foods you feel are making you sick, eliminate them from your diet for three weeks and see how much better you start to feel. Once you have more energy this will likely provide the motivation required to continue on this path of self-improvement.

Identify what areas of your life may need improving.

-How is your relationship with yourself? People who don't like themselves probably aren't very fun to be around. This isn't to say that we should love everything about ourselves; however, if we don't like ourselves then why would anyone else like us? Start by complimenting yourself daily (yes, I said daily) on all the things you like about yourself; eventually these new thoughts become automatic and you'll start to love everything about yourself.

-Are you being a good friend? It's very easy for people to say, "I have no one." This is simply because they have allowed their friends to walk all over them and have become doormats. If someone treats you poorly, politely show them the door and don't allow these negative people back into your life. You will never gain control of your happiness if you constantly let others pull you down!

-In what areas of your life do you need more energy? Energy is contagious so when we surround ourselves with positive, productive people, it's common for us to feel awake and alive! So why not surround yourself with those that make the most out of life? Start by picking up a new hobby such as exercising, eating healthier, or meditating and try to meet like-minded people via these activities.

-Are you productive? If we don't take time to prioritize our life and make daily time for important tasks, we will never be truly happy with ourselves. Even if we can only set aside 30 minutes a day, we should dedicate this time towards something truly important to us. This could be anything from learning a new language or skillset (skills add value to your character) to spending quality time with family/friends; it all comes down to prioritizing what's important in our lives!

I encourage you to tap into Stephen Covey' books, "The Seven Habits of Highly Effective People", he talks about the Quadrants of time in his Time Management Matrix. Each quadrant has a different property and is designed to help you prioritize your tasks and responsibilities. These quadrants are as follows:

- Quadrant 1: Urgent and important
- Quadrant 2: Not urgent but important

- Quadrant 3: Urgent but not important
- Quadrant 4: Not urgent and not important

We must remember that there are no perfect people in the world because everyone has room for improvement. A lot of success in life is simply being comfortable with being YOU! The moment you stop trying to be someone else is the moment people start to appreciate YOU for who YOU are.

-Identify what areas of your life may need improvement, along with a "daily commitment" for 21 days. These could include not using profanity, eating healthier, and feeling better about yourself.

-Identify the areas in which you feel you lack energy and make a daily commitment to improving them (for example exercising, meditating, or spending more time with family/friends).

-Make sure that this daily commitment lasts no longer than 30 minutes each day and prioritize those tasks that will maximize return on your investment.

-Understand that there's always room for improvement and focus on prioritizing YOU! Your happiness depends on it.

ACCEPT THE FACT THAT THERE ARE SOME THINGS IN LIFE WE CANNOT CONTROL – ONLY OURSELVES

So don't worry about it too much by trying to force something that wasn't meant to be. Changing the outcome of what you can't control will make you crazy, so focus on things in your life that are under your jurisdiction and strive for these instead of wasting energy chasing after fantasies!

An idea or thought is nothing more than a vibration or frequency of energy—it isn't real unless someone takes the time to notice it, accept it, and embrace it. Everything starts as an abstract concept until someone decides this is worth having; then they go about taking steps toward achieving their goal! You have power over how you see the world around you by choosing whether to reject or accept certain thoughts as reality! The moment you take control over your emotions and actions everything else follows suit.

Tenaciousness is the ability to withstand adversity while maintaining a positive attitude through thick and thin. This doesn't mean you should deny negativity but instead embrace it for all it's worth because every moment has something valuable to offer if you look hard enough! The more comfortable you are with discomfort the more power you have over your life because nothing can stand in your way when you're able to handle anything that comes along.

No one's perfect but this isn't an excuse to let yourself go; everything evolves by what we feed into our minds day after day—the thoughts we choose determine how our brains will ultimately interpret those thoughts as ideas, which then become things, simple as that! If we think positively then great things will come our way, but if we're negative then all we'll attract is more negativity. If you want a positive life, start by being a positive person!

A great reason for accepting negative experiences as part of the growing process is that by looking at things from this perspective, it becomes easier to see the bigger picture and realize that nothing could be any better than how it already is. It's when people stop reaching for something greater that they remain complacent with what they have— stagnation leads to death while forward momentum creates an environment ripe with infinite possibilities!

Everywhere around us has a certain vibrational frequency attached to it so if things are going wrong in your life, it's up to you to change this energy by either accepting these experiences as lessons or moving forward with a positive attitude. If you get knocked down, get back up and keep going until you reach your destination; then stop for a moment of gratitude because nothing will ever be perfect but this is no reason to give up!

Self-actualization involves making decisions from the heart instead of from what society has conditioned us to think is "correct"—the only way we can feel fulfilled is if we make choices that resonate within our hearts so why not experiment today? The world will always have negative people who try to bring us down, but it's how we choose to respond that decides our fate!

The moment you stop looking for happiness is the moment it will begin showing up in your life because when you're striving for greatness, it's only natural that greater things will follow! If you want to achieve more in life, start by being more attentive in every moment so negative thoughts won't have a place inside your head.

Everyone has their beliefs but one of the hardest things to do is embrace new ideas without feeling threatened—if something seems alien or weird it's probably because we don't understand what makes this idea different from what society has conditioned us to think is true. Education involves expanding our knowledge base by learning about all sorts of discoveries, which helps us see the bigger picture and realize that nothing can be understood unless we find ways to break expectations down into smaller pieces.

If you want to live a life full of conscious awareness then start by coming into the present moment! All moments are opportunities for change even if this change is simply an internal one where we're able to bring more awareness into our lives. It's not about being perfect but rather accepting that everything evolves in its own time, so why not embrace this fact?

The key to making positive changes in your life is through self-discipline in every moment because no matter how much you have, it will never be enough! The more aware you are of what makes you unhappy the easier it becomes to stop yourself from attracting negative experiences into your life because all energies attract when they resonate with similar frequencies— what goes around comes around!

If you want life to be easy then start by envisioning yourself as a more conscious person who can live in the moment instead of letting your mind wander. The past and future both exist inside of our heads so there's no reason why we shouldn't learn about ourselves today— why not try something new?

Every moment holds infinite possibilities even if many of them will never come true unless you make the effort to chase after them! Don't let fear hold you back because nothing feels better than setting goals for yourself and achieving them one step at a time, right? Learning how to see the world from every perspective is essential for success in any area of life.

Even when things seem bleak, that doesn't mean they'll always be this way because all of the changes in our lives start within us. Getting past these internal struggles is often challenging, but if we can get through them, everything will fall into place—nothing is ever easy but it's always worth it!

There are many more opportunities for happiness than you might realize right now, so why not try starting with one simple thing that makes you happy today? Don't listen to anyone who tries to tell you that something isn't possible; don't let fear hold you back from chasing your dreams! You aren't alone in this world, so when times get tough, reach out to family and friends.

Most problems are caused by people trying to live someone else's version of life instead of living their own, so don't be afraid to be yourself. It's not always easy, but it is necessary. We're all connected in this life so the best way to treat others is with kindness, compassion, and respect! Be mindful of your thoughts because once you learn how to recognize when negativity starts taking hold in your head, change can occur—it all starts with being conscious in every moment.

Why live this type of existence when instead you could be living a life filled with endless possibilities? Think about your actions carefully before taking them because what you put out into the universe will come back around! Everyone wants to create their unique path in life but no one ever does it alone, which is why learning from the people who have been where you are right now will help encourage you!

The more you can embrace the little things in life the happier you'll be because each moment is a gift. It's not about being perfect but rather it's about seeing yourself from another perspective and trying to create a balance between your heart and mind by being honest with both of them. There are many things that we don't understand, which is why we must always keep our minds open to new possibilities.

Every experience is a lesson if we would only take the time to notice this! If you want to live a meaningful life then start here—there's no better way to make changes than through overcoming adversity. The most valuable life lessons usually come from our mistakes so try seeing things from another person's perspective before rushing into something you might regret.

Everyone has the potential to do something great in this life if they're willing to put forth the effort—what's stopping you from making it happen? Look inside before seeking out answers because everything that we need is right here with us, waiting for us to notice it! You can't change your past but you certainly don't have to let it define who you are today, so why not start living in each moment and start over whenever necessary?

You deserve a positive and happy life filled with countless memories and amazing experiences so stop depriving yourself of what you truly want! No one else knows better than you do when it comes time to take action because only you can know what's best for yourself.

Trust in yourself and see how far you can get.

Every person has their unique talents and abilities, which is why we should all be celebrating one another's differences! There's always room for improvement, but we don't have to wait until we become perfect to start living life—there's no better time than the present. The most profound changes all begin with a single thought, so what are you thinking about today?

Sometimes it takes courage just to show up on your doorstep when your mind is telling you that it's not safe outside—remember that fear doesn't exist anywhere besides in our minds! Gather up some courage and take some risks because nothing will ever happen unless you're willing to try something new. Don't be afraid of failure because there's nothing wrong with trying and everyone has the potential to do something great if they're willing to put forth the effort.

A person's true character always comes forward under pressure so don't fall apart when things get hard! Everyone wishes that they had more time for all of their pursuits but no one ever wants to trade their health or happiness for anything, which is why it's important to stop worrying about things that are out of your control. The past is over so stop holding yourself back by allowing memories from the past to ruin your future—life is happening right now, not yesterday or tomorrow!

No matter how good or bad you might feel right now, remember that every type of situation brings some kind of lesson with it. Our job in this world isn't to be perfect but rather it's to learn from our mistakes and try again. Stop focusing on the small things that are upsetting you because, in reality, they're not that important when looking at the big picture. We only have one chance to make a positive impact in this world so why not start now?

Living life is about choosing joy every single day even if there are some bad days mixed in—no one is perfect! You can't always give people what they want but you can give them what they need, which is your time to show how much you care. The best way for us to help each other out during tough times is by being available whenever anyone needs us most. No matter how busy your life gets, your problems will never be able to run away so why not take some time out of your schedule for yourself?

No one ever said that life would be easy so why not stop making things harder than they have to be? You can only do the best that you can in any given moment, which is all that anyone can ask of you. Give yourself credit for how much progress you're making. No matter what challenges come your way, get back up and try again until you get it right because everything is a lesson that teaches us something new. Every person deserves to live life without fear or anxiety holding them back— your fears are valid but don't let them make decisions for you!

When someone tells me no, it really means "next opportunity," which gives me a chance to try later. Sometimes it's the smallest decisions that make a world of a difference—if you don't love yourself, how can anyone else? You have all this time in your life to do something great but only if you're willing to put in the work for it! Stop making excuses and take control of your life by not getting distracted from what matters. Your choices affect every single person around you so always try to treat others with kindness and respect because one day they might be gone without any notice.

Life is like an exercise machine—the more weight you want it to hold the stronger it needs to become. Be careful whom you let into your life because sometimes toxic people are drawn towards those who are easy to influence. It's better to have a few good friends than many fake ones because you can't always trust people who are quick to make promises. Your biggest problem is never going to be anything outside of your body or mind; it will always be inside of you, so do something about it! When I feel weak, I turn towards the power within me because no one else can give me strength.

Don't waste time on things that don't matter because sometimes we need to forget in order to move on. Stop spending your life worrying about your problems—remember that there are people who are struggling with real issues that are far more important than anything trivial. No amount of money will buy back the time you've lost and I'm sure you don't want to end up old, rich and miserable. The best kind of success in life is the satisfaction we get when we help someone else out. Nothing feels better than knowing that our actions have made a positive impact on another person's life.

Life is about balance so try not to take things too seriously but also remember not to be too nonchalant with your responsibilities because everything counts! Your past does not define who you are today so why would anyone want it to control their future? Everyone makes mistakes in their lives, even those who seem perfect from the outside—we're all just humans in the end. There will always be people who love and support us in this world, which is more than we could ever ask for, so take a moment to appreciate what we've been given.

Don't forget that the people in your life are only there because they love and care about you, so never take their kindness for granted. Despite how many times we fall, we always have the choice of getting back up and trying again if we believe in ourselves! No matter how low things get, no one has the power over you unless you give it to them, so don't let stress rule your life. The hardest thing in this world is holding on to someone who doesn't want to be held by us, but remember that one day our time will run out and we'll all end up alone together. It takes courage to grow up and become all that you're capable of being—you don't have to fight for what's yours if you wait long enough.

Someday, your wounds will heal and the scars that are left behind will fade into beauty because they are part of your story! What doesn't kill us only strengthens our ability to survive another day so make sure not to get too down on yourself when life gets tough. Your biggest challenges in life will force you to become a stronger person from them so never give up on who you can become or where you can go. The easiest way out is through the door but sometimes we need others' help to get back up on our feet again. I'm still learning how best to deal with my problems, but I know that time heals all wounds—don't rush things or you'll end up regretting what could've been.

Don't be too hard on yourself if you make a mistake because everyone does it from time to time! We all need love to survive so always keep your standards high because who knows whether the right person is out there waiting for you. You can't change other people but you can change how your interactions with them turn out by being kind even though they may not deserve it. It's better to take one step back and look at the bigger picture than miss something important altogether—life is full of lessons that we learn along the way, which are meant for our good.

Don't worry about things you cannot change. You must learn to adapt and overcome difficult times. When you learn to not worry too much about the things in life that are out of your control, it is easier to focus on the only thing in life you truly have control over—yourself.

THE BEST THING A PERSON CAN DO IS PREPARE FOR THE WORST BUT HOPE FOR THE BEST

You should expect everything from life—good and bad. But it's also important to be able to have faith that everything will turn out fine. This way you'll never be too disappointed or let down by life if things don't go your way all the time. It's the constant balance between taking risks and protecting yourself that will keep you grounded through it all.

Your past does not define who you are today so why would anyone want it to control their future? Letting go of the hurt, anger, or sadness from your past is harder than holding on to something that can only hurt you in the end. Once you learn how to accept what happened and move forward life becomes a lot more fun to live! You should never let other people define who you are or what you do—they aren't living your life, only you know what's best for yourself. Don't let bad habits rule your life because sooner or later they'll start controlling every aspect of who we become as people. If you want to become a better person, it's time to change some things in your life so that you start reflecting on the person you wish to be.

You can't always rely on other people to save you. It takes a lot of courage and strength to learn how to save yourself because we can only do it for ourselves when we're ready and willing. Don't let anyone push you down and hold you back from what you deserve just because they're too scared of taking a chance themselves! It's time to take control of our lives and accept the things we cannot change or might not even know about yet—this way we will never be afraid again when the truth is revealed.

We all go through hell from time to time, but it's how we make it through that journey that will define our future. There's no one way to get through every obstacle in life because everyone has a different path they must take. So, if you want things in your life to turn out the way that is best for you, then go out and fight for what you believe in! You can't always wait for other people to give you a chance—sometimes it's up to us to show them who we truly are at heart. Don't ever let anyone tell you that your dreams aren't worth pursuing or else someone else might be trying their luck on achieving something great too!

It doesn't matter where we have been when what matters is where we're going. Here is the reality, resumes tell you where I've been. How can someone define your life based on studying where you've been? If they want to understand you, they need to study where "HE" is leading you. HE said: "where I go you go"!

Life is full of new beginnings and endings, which are all equally important to our journey as individuals. We can't go back in time because there's no way to make up for things that have already happened before, so it's time to keep moving forward! Letting go of the past will always be difficult but it will help you find your new beginning, which brings with it a sense of hope for the future.

Every day is another chance at life—one more day you're here breathing on this earth. So what are you waiting for? Make today count by living life exactly how you want it without worrying too much about other people who try to bring you down. If they don't want to be part of your story then let them live their own life while you're trying to create your best work of art yet! We all have the power to do great things in this world when we work together instead of against one another.

It's always better to be an over-giver than a person who takes advantage of others. If you start by giving more than you expect in return, then good things will come back around sooner or later.

There is a book that I love and recommend, "The Go Giver", written by Bob Burg and John David Mann. It tells you to give exceptional value!

You don't need money or materialistic possessions to prove that you are good at something because good people don't need validation from others! As long as you believe in yourself and try your best every day without letting anyone get in the way then it's time for you to put your faith into action.

You can never truly know what will happen in the future if you can't even predict what may or may not happen today. Life is full of surprises and there's no way of knowing exactly what will happen next until it unfolds before us. Don't waste time worrying about what might go wrong because it won't do any good to your life; however, if you use that time to prepare yourself for anything that could happen then you'll feel a lot better once things start going right!

We all have more potential than we give ourselves credit for but we're also capable of doing a lot of damage when we don't know how to control ourselves around other people. It's important to learn how to be more patient with those who are willing to help others instead of always taking advantage of their kindness to make us feel better about ourselves. There is no reason for anyone to be mean and cruel towards others because we all deserve to live a long and happy life! It's time everyone learned about the true meaning of respect and how we could coexist with other people who are different than us as well as those who share the same beliefs as us.

It doesn't matter what kind of problems you're going through, there will always be someone else who has been in that same situation at some point in their lives. So do yourself a favor by reaching out to those around you so they can help lift your spirits and give you perspective during times when it might seem like everything is falling apart around you. The best thing you can do is keep your chin up and keep on fighting through the challenges that life throws at you every day!

Don't let your past experiences stop you from trying something new today because nobody said it would be easy to grow. All of our successes are nothing more than baby steps towards something even greater than us, so take these lessons with you as you move forward into the future. There is still so much for us all to learn, especially when it comes to the world around us—don't be afraid of stepping outside of your comfort zone no matter how many times life may knock you down.

As long as we're breathing, we should keep moving forward instead of taking one step back for every two steps forward. Life is too short to stay stuck in the past because there are so many other things for us to explore while we're still alive and kicking! It's never too late to start over again with a clean slate so don't be afraid of taking that first step into the unknown even if it means leaving something or someone behind. After all, you can always visit them one day if they decide to join you on your new adventure whenever they're ready!

Everyone has different talents and abilities but some people have it worse than others when it comes to life events. These experiences help shape our character as well as boost our self-esteem whenever we overcome adversity. If you make the best out of any given situation then life will always turn out for the better.

There's no reason to dwell on negative thoughts and feelings because you're only doing yourself a disservice whenever you let your emotions get away from you. You can't change what has already happened in the past, but it is possible to turn things around whenever you make a conscious effort to do so. Everything we do in life stems from our own choices and decisions so if there's something that is causing some problems right now then take responsibility for how it all came about by working on some solutions until they start showing results!

Tenacity isn't just the ability to bounce back after falling; it also refers to one person helping another recover from something. We can't always do everything on our own but there are a lot of other people who want to reach out and lend you a helping hand whenever you need it most. Instead of focusing on all that is bad in this world, let's try to change things around by minding our own business instead of meddling in other people's affairs.

We're all guilty of putting other people down to make ourselves feel better about our circumstances but the only ones who truly benefit from it are those thinking highly enough of themselves to keep their sanity intact! Everyone has problems, which is why we should support one another whenever someone needs help getting back up so they can be ready for whatever comes next. Don't ever forget how much power there is behind giving words of encouragement to those who are struggling with something at the moment!

You have what it takes within you to keep moving forward so never give up on reaching your goals because you deserve to be happy too. The only person standing in your way is you sometimes, but help is always available. There's no shame in asking for assistance whenever life has gotten too much for you all of a sudden. Your attitude towards other people makes all the difference in how they treat you in return, so smile instead of frowning to make the world around you a happier place to live— one step at a time!

There are times when we must march onward by ourselves without looking back or else risk falling behind completely! We can't do everything on our own sometimes but that doesn't mean we're completely on our own either. Some people are indeed self-serving but you'll find that most of them are just as lost as everyone else if they don't know how to help others feel better by making their lives easier with any given opportunity. Not everything has to be about you so stop putting your needs first all the time or else you'll soon realize that there was no real point in it!

KNOW YOUR STRENGTHS AND WEAKNESSES

Everyone has their own unique set of abilities that only they can bring to the table. Before allowing yourself to feel beaten down by life, take some time to figure out what you're good at first so you have something positive to focus on other than all the negative things that are currently making your life more difficult before it's too late!

Doing everything for yourself isn't always the best solution—sometimes other people are willing and ready to help you out whenever they can so let them hold up their end of the bargain instead of trying to do everything alone every single time! Not everyone is an expert in everything because if that was true then we would all be doing the same thing as one another without encountering any issues whatsoever along the way. People will always need help sometimes so don't be afraid to ask for it yourself when the time is right!

Sometimes we must reach deep within ourselves just to discover our inner strength. There's no shame in needing a little bit of support from someone else whenever you're not feeling strong enough to do something on your own without any help whatsoever because we've all been there at some point before. Life never stops throwing obstacles in our paths so we must learn how to work around them without letting them bring us down completely. Stay positive and things will work themselves out if you take the time to reflect upon how far you've already come as well as where you're headed next!

We've all got good points and bad points about ourselves that we need to embrace when we're struggling with something and can't find a way out on our own. Don't let the opinions of other people dictate how you feel about yourself because what they say isn't always true! If you don't believe in yourself then no one else will either, so be your own biggest supporter whenever life gets too much for you to handle without falling apart. There's nothing wrong with needing help from time to time but don't forget where your strengths lie either!

DRAW UP A PLAN FOR WHAT YOU WANT TO ACHIEVE AND HOW IT WILL AFFECT YOUR LIFE

Few people can achieve anything worthwhile without any sort of plan whatsoever. There's no point in dreaming about how great your future can be if you can't do anything about it right now—start planning for the things you want the most! Maybe you don't know where to begin, but once you've figured out what your ultimate goal is it will be much easier for you to formulate a plan of action for how to get there. Whether or not you believe everything happens for a reason, creating plans is necessary whenever we want something badly enough otherwise life will pass us by before we even realize what's happening!

Don't expect everyone else around you to understand your dreams and ambitions because they won't unless they're just as passionate about them as you are. That's why it's important to surround yourself with like-minded people whenever possible or else you might start giving up on your dreams without even realizing it! Stay focused and follow through with whatever plan was set out for you—the rest will sort itself out along the way if you never give up on what truly matters most to you.

Feelings of envy, greed, and selfishness can be detrimental so try not to let them affect your life too much unless they're justifiable in some way. If someone is getting ahead of themselves then it's your job to remind them that there's no need to pull everyone else down around them just because they're having a good time. We all have one life to live so don't destroy the achievements of others because you'll never be happy once that happens. Being a caring person means being able to take time out for yourself whenever you need it without trying to rely on anyone else too much.

Change is a part of life so we must learn how to embrace it when it comes our way instead of running away from every new challenge in our lives. Don't worry about things going wrong because they can always be put back together again— it's not easy but at least everything will feel more worthwhile when all the hard work has been done! Sometimes change comes into our lives for a reason and we must be prepared to go with the flow wherever possible even if there's some resistance at first; just keep reminding yourself that nothing good comes easy in life so the sooner you stop thinking that way the better off you'll be.

Don't let other people tell you what to do or how to think because you're just as important as anyone else who has ever been alive—stand up for yourself and defend your rights no matter what the cost! It's not easy being a strong person, but if it was everyone would be able to achieve their dreams without having to worry about what others thought of them along the way. Being an independent thinker means making your own choices based on what feels right at any given moment even when those around you don't necessarily agree with your views, which is why we need to surround ourselves with like-minded people whenever possible. Never back down from your convictions and always do what you feel is right in your heart because it's how we truly express who we are when all is said and done.

COMMIT TO THIS NEW ROUTINE, EVEN IF IT'S HARD AT FIRST

There's no better feeling than looking back on all of the progress you've made!

Introducing a new routine can be tough at first, but with time and practice you'll become used to it. It's such a rewarding feeling when you look back on all of the progress you've made!

Tenaciousness is your ability to bounce back from whatever life throws at you—those things that make us question who we are, what we stand for, and why we're here.

Having a strong inner resolve and belief in oneself is critical to developing a spirit of tenacity. When tragedy strikes and the world around us falls apart, our perceived notions of reality can shatter as well. The only thing that remains constant is one's perception; it may vanish momentarily but will return just as fast.

This is where our tenaciousness comes in—it's the voice in the back of your head telling you to get up when life knocks you down. It's what convinces us that things will be okay no matter how dire they may seem. When challenges come, they tell us that we can persevere and emerge with strength befitting a warrior. No obstacle is insurmountable, no tragedy permanent.

When wading through difficult times, one must find personal meaning within their pain. This allows us to grow from our struggles instead of succumbing to them. Yes, even negative things carry positive lessons but only if we allow ourselves to see them as such.

Having tenaciousness does not mean we will never encounter setbacks, but whatever comes our way, we can overcome it. It means that no matter how hard life gets, there's always a solution and an end to the struggle is in sight.

It also means that upon encountering problems you're better equipped to handle them with grace and dignity because you're aware of your limitations as well as your strengths. It all boils down to whether or not we let external forces affect our internal state of being. A person with a strong inner resolve is less likely to lose their cool over trivial matters—they may still become frustrated or angry, but they won't freak out about small issues as many do. In other words, they acknowledge and accept their emotions without letting them control them.

In a world where we're constantly being judged by how much money we have or what our job title is, it's important to develop a healthy sense of self-esteem that causes you to value who you are instead of your possessions, accomplishments, or what other people think about you. Having high expectations of yourself can be beneficial but only if they don't become so lofty that impossibility becomes the standard. If you expect perfection from your abilities while simultaneously ignoring your shortcomings, no amount of positive thinking will help because you'll be setting yourself up for failure every single time. It's far more productive to be kind towards yourself and embrace all aspects of life—both good and bad—as they come.

Also, you must learn to love yourself before loving others. If you aren't at peace with who you are as a person, how can anyone else bring that out in you? No one is perfect but everyone has the power to become better versions of themselves—that's ultimately what being human is all about: finding areas for improvement and then working hard to attain those goals. Life will never be a fairy tale so don't expect it to be—remember that even Snow White had a wicked stepmother! Instead of asking why life is so unfair, ask questions like, "What have I learned from this?" or, "How can I grow from my experiences?" You can persevere because you're stronger than you think.

Ultimately, having a spirit of tenacity is about choosing to see the glass as half full. It acknowledges that no matter how bad things may seem there's always something positive you can take away from them (i.e. opportunities for personal development). Negative emotions are unavoidable but they don't have to be negative experiences—every misfortune holds within it an opportunity for us to learn and grow as people so why not seek out those lessons? Make lemonade out of lemons because life will never stop giving you lemons! When confronted with adversity, think back on what your parents told you when you were growing up: "Someday this will all be just a passing memory."

TIME WAITS FOR NO ONE

Time is a non-replenishable asset. Once it's spent you can never get it back.

You can't control how time flies but you can control how much time you spend doing something that matters to you—don't waste it on regrets that won't matter tomorrow, so why wait until later today? No matter how hard times get, remember not to take yourself back too far because your past does not define who you are today so why keep reliving it? You can't undo any mistakes you've made but if you learn from them, they're worth more than all the success in the world because success without knowledge is pointless.

Sometimes life doesn't turn out how we want it to so instead of moping around and complaining about how unfair things are, ask yourself what you can do now to make things better. It might be hard to see through the fog at first, but as long as you don't give up completely there's always a way to make your dreams come true! One day at a time will get anyone across the finish line so keep going even when things seem impossible.

Every day is a new chance to seize opportunities before they slip away forever! Even though you can't change the past, you do shape your future so don't waste it away by licking your wounds and dwelling on things you can never undo. Life is about learning from mistakes so instead of living in regret, live in the present moment because there's no telling what tomorrow might bring! The past may be important but that doesn't mean it should define how we act today—just because something has happened to us doesn't mean that it must happen to everyone else too!

Don't let negative emotions get the best of you because they're nothing more than toxins that fester inside our bodies until they make us sick (mentally if not physically). Not allowing yourself to experience negative feelings like anxiety or stress only leads to discomfort at some point because ignoring your fears doesn't make them go away—it makes them harder to control. So instead of bottling up negative emotions, learn how to channel them into something more productive! You can always find ways to turn lessons into life-changing opportunities if you give yourself the chance to think things through before reacting. Every cloud has a silver lining so wait for it and once you see what it is, grab on to that opportunity with both hands.

Never say never but don't expect things to happen overnight either! Although setting goals isn't a bad thing, it's important not to forget about all the other little steps in between achieving those milestones! What matter most are efforts rather than results so be patient with yourself while still holding yourself accountable for going after what you want out of life. There will always be people who have achieved more than you but there will also be those who have done less, so instead of letting the jealousy eat away at your heart, focus on how much potential there is left to unlock! You can never accomplish everything all at once but that doesn't mean you should stop trying—remember that nothing good ever comes from giving up either!

THINK POSITIVELY ABOUT YOURSELF AND OTHERS AROUND YOU

Everyone has their weaknesses; you cannot take notice of those people who are negative about themselves and the world they live in every day because you don't want them to drag you down with them.

CHAPTER 9

ANCHOR YOURSELF
IN FAITH

Resilience is a spirit of hope because we trust that we can endure all things; we believe that we will make it through tough challenges. We must place our faith in God—He who projects His love into our hearts like beams of light—and be anchored by all that is spiritual: prayer and meditation, Scripture reading, and living out the Word daily. God has promised us many blessings for obeying Him so let's put our hopes on those promises and not our insecurities. We need God to walk us through the difficult times of our lives.

Do you know the story of Joash? He became king at seven years old. As a boy, he had to endure many hardships—from his mother plotting against him to being kidnapped by people who tried to poison him. Even though he was surrounded by bad influences, his faith in God allowed him to overcome all the obstacles that were placed before him. His power of tenaciousness was anchored in his faith in God.

As you face challenges or trials in your life, remember this truth: God is always with you whatever situation you are facing because He has promised never to leave or forsake us (Hebrews 13:5). No matter how difficult the trial may be, if you have committed yourself into His hands and anchored your spirit in faith, you will have the power to overcome.

DEVELOP A SENSE OF GRATITUDE

Another way to develop grit is by developing a "sense of gratitude"—a statement that would normally be considered contradictory. However, many who are bouncy dwell on what they are grateful for rather than what they lack. They remain positive by focusing on two important things: (1) their blessings and (2) God's love and care for them. You can develop and increase your sense of thankfulness and appreciation by examining every situation with the eye of truth. Make it a habit to look at all your experiences from God's perspective; acknowledge His presence and goodness and see how He has taken care of you even in difficult times.

There are times when you might feel that you do not have anything to be grateful about, but if you look closely enough—if you are willing to see beyond your current situation—you will find many reasons for thankfulness in your life. Remember the words of Ralph Waldo Emerson: "For everything you have missed, you have gained something else; and for everything you gain, you lose something else."

▪ BE READY TO BOUNCE BACK

Resiliency involves bouncing back from setbacks and negativity. The key to bouncing back is in the power of tenacity—you need it when times get rough so that things will not knock you out completely. Practicing tenaciousness means putting up a good fight because we know that winning or overcoming obstacles will bring us much joy and happiness.

Many people give up when they experience rejection or failure but resilient ones keep looking ahead no matter what might come their way. They look at clouds with silver linings instead of the dark side of the clouds because they are determined to overcome them.

Developing tenaciousness requires us to be proactive in our decision-making, taking into consideration that there are consequences for each choice we make not only for ourselves but also for those around us, which is the same idea as practicing responsibility. Instead of getting angry or disappointed with people because they did something you might not approve of, try seeing their side of the picture and learn how you can deal with these situations more productively.

Before entering a situation or expressing your feelings about it, always take time to think carefully about what you want to say and do so within God's will. This way, you won't say or do anything out of anger and frustration and you will find yourself reacting wisely during difficult times (Colossians 4:6). And because you have made wise choices, you will never go wrong and will always be blessed in the process.

"I was ready for anything and confident I could deal with whatever came my way." - Derek Jeter

The power of developing tenaciousness is possible when we consciously decide to put into practice what we know instead of just thinking about it. It is not just a matter of standing up again after falling but rising higher than where we were before. Resilient people are determined to cope with life's difficulties even though they may resist some things at first. Being bouncy takes some conscious effort on your part—it does not happen overnight nor will it come easily all the time. Sometimes, you may feel weak or overwhelmed, but if you are willing to be open to God's guidance, He will give you the strength and courage needed for you to bounce back from life's disappointments.

The power of developing tenaciousness is possible only through the help of God—He will never leave us nor forsake us (Deuteronomy 31:6). If we continue to have faith in Him despite our struggles, He will bless us with His presence, which gives us hope, especially during difficult times. When we experience failure or rejection, again and again, this should not stop us from believing that things can change because anything is possible if we trust in His unfailing love for all people (Jeremiah 29:11).

The power in developing a spirit of resiliency can be ours when we allow God to take charge of our lives and guide us towards the path where He is. It will not be easy but God promises us that if we seek Him first (Matthew 6:33), we will discover that trusting in His unfailing love for all people and relying on His guidance and wisdom (James 1:5–6) will bring the life we want. So don't give up—there is always light at the end of every tunnel!

Trust in the LORD with all your heart and lean not on your understanding; In all your ways submit to him, and he will make your paths straight. Do not be wise in your own eyes; fear the LORD and shun evil. This will bring health to your body and nourishment to your bones. Proverbs 3:5–8

Bible verses about developing grit (and similar ideas):

Proverbs 24:16 - A righteous man may suffer many troubles, but the LORD delivers him from them all; 2 Timothy 1:7 - For God has not given us a spirit of fear, but of power and love and a sound mind; James 1:12–15 - Blessed is the man who perseveres under trial because when he has stood the test, he will receive the crown of life that God has promised to those who love him. When tempted, no one should say, "God is tempting me." For God cannot be tempted by evil, nor does he tempt anyone; but each person is tempted when they are dragged away by their evil desire and enticed. Then, after desire has conceived, it gives birth to sin; and sin, when it is full-grown, gives birth to death.

Romans 8:28 - And we know that in all things God works for the good of those who love him, who have been called according to his purpose.

2 Corinthians 12:9 - But he said to me, "My grace is sufficient for you, for my power is made perfect in weakness." Therefore, I will boast all the more gladly about my weaknesses, so that Christ's power may rest on me.

Philippians 4:13 - I can do all this through him who gives me strength. NOTE: This means we can learn how to develop tenacity by putting our trust in Him and He will show us what we need to learn and do to become resilient people!

Remember that your mind is powerful and you can develop tenaciousness if you choose to do so, aligning yourself with God's will for your life! A positive attitude not only affects how you respond when things go wrong but it also transcends into other aspects of your life, positively shaping the way others see you too.

And whatever happens, [if] God [is] with [you], nothing [can] happen to you without God's will.

Embrace each day one step at a time.

We all have big dreams, but just like uprooting plants too early can kill them or stop their growth, disruption can do the same for our progress in life. The best way to keep moving forward is to stay calm and focused on what we can do today, not worrying about what might happen tomorrow. Some days may take more effort than others, but if we get up with the strength and courage to press on knowing that God has already given us everything we need for the challenges ahead of us, then there should be nothing standing in our way! Embrace each day one step at a time so that when you look back, you'll see how far you've come!

▌ PUT YOUR HOPE IN GOD ALONE

Don't be too quick to give up on people. In life, there are going to be people who will let us down but they're not letting us down because we have value or we matter. We may feel that being let down is a reflection of our self-worth and even a confirmation that no one would choose, but it's just a reflection of the poor decisions of others and/or their lack of understanding of how to conduct themselves in relationships. But don't stop believing in people; instead, put your hope in God alone because He is the One who can turn this situation around for good (Jeremiah 29:11).

▌ LEAVING SPACE FOR GOD'S PRESENCE IN YOUR LIFE IS KEY TO DEVELOPING RESILIENCY

Developing a spirit of tenacity starts with making room for God's presence in our hearts. This isn't something that God can give us; it's not magic, but it does require humility and obedience because the only way we will be able to experience His love and feel closer to Him is if we keep our eyes on Him (Hebrews 12:2). That means putting aside all distractions like sin, pride, negative thoughts, wrong attitudes, and unforgiveness— anything that would take us away from what He has for us. If we choose to cling on to those things then they will act like weights that are holding us down. We have to release them so that we can be free to run and jump for joy!

Developing strength of character takes time, but it's like practicing scales on the piano; you must keep at it if you ever want to play a beautiful melody that touches hearts. It's hard work, but in due season you will see that your efforts are paying off (Galatians 6:9). So hang in there; don't give up even though times may get tough because with God all things are possible (Matthew 19:26).

KEEP MOVING FORWARD NO MATTER WHAT HAPPENS

No matter how many times we fall or fail or make poor choices, God is always ready to forgive us and help us start over again (1 John 1:9). But after we receive His forgiveness it's up to us to decide if we want to make the same mistakes again or learn from them and choose not to fall into temptation. On our own, it can be difficult to resist temptation, but with God on our side He will give us the strength that we need (Matthew 11:28–30). Don't hesitate; don't worry; just keep moving forward no matter what happens because God always has a plan for good in store for you (Genesis 50:20)!

DON'T LET FEAR STOP YOU!

We all want self-confidence but too often Satan can plant thoughts of doubt in our heads. "What if you fail?" "What if you're not good enough?" "Maybe you should just give up." These are the kinds of questions we need to silence because no matter what we're going through, we must stay focused on God and all that He has already given us (Hebrews 12:2). Besides, fear doesn't come from God so don't let it stop you from pursuing your dreams! It's time to take a stand against the devil!

GOD ALONE FILLS OUR HEARTS WITH HOPE

The best way to resist the devil is by keeping busy doing things for God. Every morning, when you wake up, ask Him to fill your heart with His hope and courage so that you can have a productive day. Ask God to help you avoid temptations and people who would try to lead you astray. When we build a strong relationship with God, He will provide the strength and the ability to always do what is right (2 Peter 1:3–4).

BE PATIENT WITH YOURSELF

We need to learn how to care for ourselves so we can better cope with life's challenges. We must forgive ourselves when we don't meet expectations and try again. Our impatience makes us prone to feeling frustration, anger, and resentment, which defeat resilience; they lead to depression and we become worn down by every little thing that happens. We must realize it is okay to be human and allow ourselves grace when we fall short because this isn't a contest: there is no prize for the most resilient but at least you will have good memories of your struggle on the way towards finding your way through tough times.

We also need to understand the nature of our problems, their source, and how they impact us as individuals as well as within a group or family unit (or whatever social structures we are involved in). What needs to be done is an honest assessment based on facts and truth because sometimes we can cast similar problems into different dark shadows; we see certain events as more difficult than they are and it becomes a self-fulfilling prophecy: all that glitters is not gold. Once we check for any inherent biases then the sky won't seem like it's falling just because someone disagrees with us.

Finally, if you feel overwhelmed by life's challenges then take some time off to regroup without feeling guilty because you need a break from all of the pressure in your life. God never intended for us to work ourselves to death and neglect our own needs; we are not machines, we have limitations! Breathe deeply. God is faithful and He will provide whatever it is that you need when you return to being fully engaged with what's going on around you again.

MOVE FORWARD FROM LOSS WITH CONFIDENCE

In life, there will be failures as well as successes, some of which will be more painful than others. We have all had personal experiences with loss and it can be paralyzing to move forward. But there is a way out of the darkness. When we feel stuck in mourning, it's helpful to remember these three steps: (1) Make a conscious decision to get up and start moving again; (2) look to God for comfort; (3) don't let what you've lost steal who you are now.

BUILD YOUR WILL LIKE TEMPERED STEEL

To build your spirit and master self-mastery, you must tap into your inner strength and tenacity like tempered steel, strong and flexible at the same time. The following four tools will help: (1) Fasting to strengthen your spirit; (2) Mental focus on exercising the mental muscle of self-control; (3) Physical activity to build endurance and energy through movement, which is a form of meditation; (4) Studying God's Word daily to get pumped up with positive thinking.

■ BECOME AN ALL-WEATHER FRIEND

The best way to make new friends is by being an all-weather friend yourself! An all-weather friend is someone who stands by you through thick and thin, always ready for the next get-together. My challenge to you is simple: be that person for others. Extend your hand in friendship often and approach people with humility rather than pride because no one likes a know-it-all or someone who tries to show off to the other person.

■ BE A FORCE FOR GOOD IN THE WORLD

When you are whippy, you are tough enough to stand tall against any challenges that come your way. You won't be changed—you will still be you, inside and out. The world needs people like you who can make it through tough times without losing faith or hope in yourself or others around you. So, remind yourself often of this truth: "I possess the strength to transcend my circumstances." This is your power because people need us now more than ever!

CHAPTER 10

EXERCISE YOUR STRENGTH MUSCLE

Steps to build your resilience muscle

Steps to building up your resilience muscle.

Early traumatic experiences work for you as you learn how to adapt earlier in life.

For example, breathing during a difficult situation to keep yourself alive/calm helps you remember what is important in life even if it is about surviving.

Using others as a resource, for example a mentor.

Taking a break from the situation that is causing you difficulty to regain your strength/energy.

And finally practicing positive thinking and knowing healthy coping strategies; for example, if something stresses you out, talk it through with someone or do some deep breathing exercises.

Tenacity builds over time. If a life event happens, but the person comes out stronger than before, this is building the resiliency muscle (scientists call it stress inoculation). The more they build up these muscles the less susceptible they are to depression or anxiety.

Everything happens for a reason—sometimes things go wrong that could be the most stressful thing ever; however, understanding everything allows us to grow as people.

Once you realize that all of your experiences, good and bad alike, are opportunities to learn about yourself it is possible to see an unfortunate event as something helpful to internal development. For example, if there was a time when you got into trouble at school or with the law, this would be an opportunity for growth because it helps you explore what mistakes you made and how not to make them again in the future.

Everyone needs support throughout life; after early traumatic experiences like divorce parents or the death of someone close can help. One way people deal with challenges is to reframe the experience by saying "putting myself in their shoes," which helps people grow by relating to things that happened to other people who went through similar situations (even though it did not happen to them).

Taking a break from a stressful situation gives us time to regain our energy and strength while also having the opportunity for privacy and reflection. This is important when dealing with stress because too much strain on your emotional/physical stability can be harmful in the long term.

Positive thinking allows you to focus on what you can change about yourself, rather than focusing on what is wrong with the world around you—it helps build tenaciousness by realizing that we do have control over both internal and external situations. Being able to cope with any challenge in life builds grit muscles through the practice of healthy coping strategies such as deep breathing exercises, talking something out with people who care, etc.

Exercising muscles is not always easy, but it builds the body/mind stronger. If you do not exercise a muscle that you build up it can be weakened over time. Caring for yourself and your mental wellbeing will help to build grit.

Being resilient means overcoming internal and external obstacles. It means being able to still think positively even when going through unfortunate experiences or feeling overwhelmed with stress. Research has shown that this type of behavior changes brain structure, which helps control impulses and emotions more effectively so people are less likely to relapse into depression, anxiety, etc. Grit allows people to take responsibility for themselves as they go through life challenges by knowing what they can do better next time instead of having negative thought processes.

IDENTIFY A STRONG MUSCLE THAT YOU WANT TO BUILD UP

I chose the muscle of mindfulness. Mindfulness means being aware of what is happening around you and how to react to it positively. Imagine that your body is like clay; every new experience, good or bad, adds another layer onto you, which shapes who you are as a person. Mindfulness allows you to act with intention instead of reacting (like an uncontrolled volcano eruption) without thinking about what happens. For example: if someone were to make fun of me, mindfulness would allow me to acknowledge my feelings but not let them control my actions (becoming reactionary). This creates tenacity because I can take responsibility for myself by acting out how I want to (not letting others' words affect whether or not I say something back to them). When I act with intention, it helps me grow as a person because I am actively practicing responding to bad things rather than just letting them happen. Mindfulness is like building muscles, but you have to practice every single day or else it will weaken over time. Mindfulness builds up your emotional wellbeing by learning how to focus on what you can do better next time instead of becoming overwhelmed with negative thoughts/feelings.

For example: If someone calls you fat, mindfulness wants you to acknowledge that hurtful word and your feelings towards it (ex. sad/mad) without saying anything back that might escalate the situation. Instead of proactively looking for opportunities to fight with that person and becoming reactionary, mindfulness would teach you that you can't control what they say but you can control how you let it affect your emotions. Mindfulness does not want to allow those types of situations to ruin your self-esteem because we know they don't define who you are as a person.

I am building this muscle by keeping a gratitude journal so I write down one to three things every day that I am grateful for/happy about. This helps me focus on the positive aspects of my life instead of dwelling on the negative. It also makes me more mindful by using descriptive words and details about each aspect, which allows me to recall them easily and practice mindfulness every time I read my journal entries later on in the day or week.

Being resilient means overcoming internal and external obstacles. It means being able to still think positively even when going through unfortunate experiences or feeling overwhelmed with stress. Research has shown that this type of behavior changes brain structure, which helps control impulses and emotions more effectively so people are less likely to relapse into depression, anxiety, etc. Grit allows people to take responsibility for themselves as they go through life's challenges by knowing what they can do better next time instead of having negative thought processes.

BENEFITS OF DEVELOPING A SPIRIT/ TENACITY IN BUILDING UP THIS MUSCLE.

1. "Positive thinking" is an example of good coping strategies in dealing with stress because it allows people to focus on what they can change about

themselves when going through challenging situations instead of focusing on the bad things around them.

2. Practicing deep breathing exercises when feeling overwhelmed by life's difficulties will help develop control over impulses and emotions so people are less likely to relapse into depression, anxiety, etc. Studies have shown changes in brain structure through practicing resiliency, which helps control impulses and emotions more effectively.

3. Taking a break from difficult situations allows time for the person to regain their energy and strength while also having the opportunity for privacy and reflection. This is important when dealing with stress because too much strain on your emotional/physical stability can be harmful in the long term.

4. Therapy has been shown to increase self-awareness of an individual's internal conflicts as well as prompt them to find healthier ways of coping with anxiety and depression. Coping skills such as deep breathing exercises, talking to someone who cares about you, etc., help build grit muscles through practice so people are less likely to relapse into depression or other problems associated with it.

5. Developing tenaciousness means overcoming internal and external obstacles. It means being able to still think positively even when going through unfortunate experiences or feeling overwhelmed with stress, which helps develop control over impulses and emotions more effectively so people

are less likely to relapse into depression, anxiety, etc. Tenacity allows people to take responsibility for themselves as they go through life's challenges by knowing what they can do better next time instead of having negative thought processes. This ultimately changes brain structure, which helps control impulses and emotions more effectively.

STEPS TO BUILDING UP YOUR RESILIENCE MUSCLE

1. Recognize when your wellbeing is being challenged because these are the times when you need grit most.

2. Ask yourself how your wellbeing is being challenged to determine if it's internal or external because this allows you to figure out what kind of support you need in coping with the challenge(s).

3. Ask someone for their help when dealing with challenges so they can provide emotional stability, which will prevent negative thought processes and relapse into depression/anxiety, etc.

4. Take a break from these challenging situations periodically to regain energy and strength while also giving yourself privacy and reflection time for a better understanding of where you are emotionally/physically. Reflecting on whether these difficult experiences are internal or external and what kind of support you need will help with

coping strategies such as deep breathing exercises, talking to someone who cares about you, etc.

5. Practice these healthy coping strategies so they become second nature and more readily available for challenging situations. By practicing healthy coping strategies, people can reduce their chances of relapse and give themselves a better chance of overcoming the obstacles they face in life. This ultimately changes brain structure, which helps control impulses and emotions more effectively. Tenacity enables people to take responsibility for themselves as they go through life's challenges by knowing what they can do better next time instead of having negative thought processes.

CHAPTER 11

THE TEST – OPPORTUNITY TO GROW OR SHRINK

Ask yourself if you are using any experience to grow or shrink. Are you giving in to fear or moving forward in the spirit and knowing that this thing is happening FOR you? You have the capacity and you are powerful enough to turn anything into something that works for you. We all can do this. All of us feel fear, but we can learn how to transmute that fear into faith. You are learning from everything you experience in your life.

THE TEST IS AN OPPORTUNITY TO GROW OR SHRINK

We are all in the process of either growing or shrinking. We are always using manifestation, either for good or bad. There is no evil spirit making us do things (evil does not exist). It's our consciousness that chooses between whether we will grow or shrink. Everything you experience in life can be used for your benefit if you want to use it that way.

Grit is the ability to bounce back. We all go through difficult times and we can train ourselves to become more resilient so that these times don't define us as much as they used to. It doesn't mean that we learn nothing from those situations, but we learn how to acknowledge what happened and let it go quickly. There's a sense of "Whew!" not only because you've survived but because you're ready for whatever comes next and maybe even using it as an opportunity for growth.

RESILIENCY – ABILITY TO BEND WITHOUT BREAKING

The only way you can be strong is by allowing yourself to express emotion because when you hold back your tears, you become hard inside and this blocks feelings of love from coming out towards others. The same thing happens with anger, sadness, disappointment... When these emotions build up inside of us, they block off love energy, which causes us to feel isolated.

Bending without breaking means that we can take the tests and opportunities thrown at us in life and make them work for us rather than against us. We can choose to bend but not break when something bad happens to us or when we face a test in our lives. This is about redirecting your thoughts and realigning your emotions (which makes you spiritual). It's about finding within you the strength to carry on through hard times and finding positivity in every situation no matter how difficult it seems at the time.

GROWTH MINDSET VS. SHRINKING MINDSET

The growth mindset simply means that you can take something difficult and find opportunities in it. It's about changing your thought process so you think of the possibilities instead of focusing on the negatives. If something doesn't work out or if there is a problem, you choose to see it as an opportunity for growth rather than seeing yourself as a victim who didn't get what they wanted.

Write down everything that makes you angry and read over it at least once every day for two weeks. After two weeks, go through this list again and highlight all the things you can do anything about now vs. those that are out of your control (the latter should be crossed off). Everything else must be moved to the first category because if we focus intensely on stuff we can't do anything about now, it will make us feel powerless and stop us from changing things that need to be changed.

It's important to keep your emotions in check because you have the power to manifest everything you want. It's about using your mind constructively instead of destructively by focusing on what makes you happy rather than what makes you sad or angry. What are the signals that tell you which thoughts are good or bad? Any time your feelings are hurt or someone is not nice to you, this is a sign that something isn't aligned with love energy so don't give any power to those thoughts. We can choose our response instead of being pushed around by people who push our buttons because these people only exist in our minds.

When you become aware that you're thinking about something that is not aligned with love energy, shift your thoughts to something else. There are so many good things around us all the time so choose to focus on those instead of what's making you feel bad! You can do this by finding beauty or abundance everywhere, even if it doesn't seem like it at first. If you look for opportunities to connect with nature outside, this will help align your thoughts with peace and harmony, which will cause change within you. Doing this causes positive changes within others as well because energy follows thought. This means that whatever we think radiates into the world around us and other people pick up on it whether they realize it or not.

▌ STEPS TO SHIFTING YOUR THOUGHTS:

1. Identify what you are thinking about at the moment.
2. Find out whether it's an opportunity for growth or not.
3. If it is, carry on with this thought and find opportunities within that situation; if it isn't, then

stop thinking about it now because dwelling on anything negative will only make things worse.

4. Shift your thought to something positive instead of focusing on the negatives over and over again, which will make you feel powerless. You can do this by picking out the little things that make you happy and emphasizing those instead.

5. Keep doing this over and over again until it becomes a habit and you always choose to think positive thoughts rather than negative ones. Any time your thoughts drift back into negativity, remember steps 1 through 5! Remember to have fun with this process because you are making changes within you so enjoy it!

The shrinking mindset makes us feel terrible about ourselves by putting us down whenever anything doesn't go our way or if someone criticizes us even in the slightest bit. It's important to stop focusing on the negative stuff. After all, it only causes pain, which will become more intense as time goes by no matter how much we try to ignore/forget about it.

What does the power of this mindset come from? The power of grit comes from thinking like a warrior and seeing life as an adventure rather than letting things get to us because we'll only waste time worrying about stuff when we should instead be focusing on approaching things positively; by doing this, we can accomplish great feats! A good way to shift your perspective is by using the world around you for inspiration or watching uplifting documentaries. You are able to choose who you want to be in life rather than being forced into situations with people who don't align themselves with love energy.

Identify what inspires you most (because it's likely related to your purpose) and follow that passion wherever it takes you! If there's nothing that inspires you then figure out what can. This is your purpose, so stop ignoring it by trying to do something else with your life! Your purpose will make you truly happy because doing things we love brings happiness from within, which no one or thing from outside can ever take away from us!

Being a victim makes people unconsciously choose not to try as hard as they could be because they think they can't accomplish their dreams if they don't have the 'right looks'/ status/connections, etc... However, everyone has potential regardless of how much money/ power/fame they have.

You need to view failure as an opportunity for growth rather than something scary or bad. Adversity helps us grow stronger if we allow it to; therefore, always keep trying despite all odds against you. Just like Thomas Jefferson once said, "I am a great believer in luck and I find that the harder I work, the more I have of it!"

Remember to be grateful because it makes you happier. It's easy for us to say we're grateful but it means nothing if your words don't match up with your actions so always keep track of what you are saying because people tend to say things they don't mean especially during moments when they feel upset/ stressed/anxious, etc... If you are aware that this is happening then all you need to do is stop yourself from saying those things! When something happens that causes you to behave badly, go outside/take a walk until you cool down or try doing something positive like reading a book.

Remember to get enough sleep; it's important because when we get tired, our brains don't work properly, which makes us feel like we can't accomplish anything. Make sure you go to bed early (10:00–11:00 p.m.) and wake up early (4:00–6:00 a.m.) every day; if not then try to at least sleep for six or seven hours every night!

The power of this mindset comes from thinking like a warrior and seeing life as an adventure rather than letting things get to us because we'll only waste time worrying about stuff when we should instead be focusing on approaching things positively; by doing this, you accomplish great feats! You are able to choose who you want to be in life rather than being forced into situations with people who don't align themselves with love energy.

There are two types of people in this world: glass half empty, glass half full. If you have a glass half empty mindset then you will always see the negative aspects of life rather than the positive ones because that's what your brain focuses on since it's more used to seeing things that way. However, if you have a glass half full mindset then you are thinking positively, which makes you feel better about everything!

To have a glass half full outlook on life all you need to do is think right now, What do I have? How many people would kill for this opportunity/experience? Stop thinking, Why is this happening? How did my plans get ruined? because when you think like that, your brain releases chemicals that make you feel bad.

If you are wondering what to do after a certain event happens then ask yourself, I wonder...? and let your imagination fill in the blanks as opposed to thinking about all the possibilities of failure because those thoughts won't help at all! Learn from those who have already done it before you so you know what not to do, etc.

If you have an interest/hobby then google how to advance your skills in that certain area! There are countless numbers of articles written on how people can advance their abilities to take advantage of them if they are willing to put in the work. Developing talent is something that takes time so don't expect everything overnight, especially when someone tells you, "I'm going to be a professional dancer by next week!" because chances are they won't achieve anything close to being successful.

You should always work on your strengths rather than focusing on your weaknesses because if you constantly try to fix your flaws, chances are very low that you'll be successful even if you do manage to make progress. You can always build off of self-perceived success and learn from mistakes.

Let's say there is something difficult/hard about being an astronaut so instead of dwelling so much on being one or finding out how hard it is, just imagine being one! Look at the positive side by imagining what it feels like so you can get motivated enough to do this! Remember, there are no mistakes in life only learning experiences. You can't have a positive mind frame if you don't believe that happiness is your right, so try embracing the fact that whatever happens, good or bad, is all a part of life's journey!

The more you focus on everything being a part of this wonderful experience called life then the better off you'll be because people who think negatively won't have many memories to look back on or anything they feel passionate about doing. They will live with regrets because they didn't get what they wanted so instead of trying different things out for fun, they just wasted their time thinking, What if? which will never bring them anywhere...

Some people are negative but don't realize it because their subconscious mind is in control of that. What your subconscious mind does and what you are aware of are two different things.

Also, if something doesn't feel right then it probably isn't, so trust your instincts! People who make the wrong decision tend to be more stressed out than others when they realize their mistake but since they trusted themselves at that moment they felt relieved because it did feel right! Being able to know what's best for you will give you confidence/trust in yourself, which then allows you to take chances with anything you do in life.

What people don't know is that negative thoughts increase stress because the part of the brain called the amygdala controls our emotional reactions, so if your amygdala decides to convert a stressful event into a memory, then your mind will be in stress mode for the next couple of days or even weeks! So, try not to build up any negative thoughts because that will eventually take its toll on you.

- Positive people are happier because they focus on everything amazing about life instead of focusing on what's wrong with their situation; also, they tend to look at difficulties as an opportunity to grow and learn something new (which is fun/exciting). They keep trying because they know there isn't anything worth regretting.
- Negative people are more stressed out than others if things don't go according to plan; but if things do work out for them, they make excuses so chances are they will never be successful.
- Everyone makes mistakes; there are no mistakes in life only learning experiences. So, if you think something is hard then picture yourself doing that thing but imagine how good it feels to achieve your goal! If it doesn't feel right then chances are it's not for you so don't hurt yourself by trying... Just live in the moment and enjoy whatever hobby/interests you have without having expectations all the time because those who expect less tend to get more (life isn't always fair)!
- People should always work on their strengths rather than focusing too much on fixing their flaws because if people focus on fixing what's wrong with them they won't find time to do anything fun/productive, which will cause even more stress.

- Everyone should embrace the fact that whatever happens, good or bad, is all a part of life's journey! The more you focus on everything being a part of this wonderful experience called life then the better off you'll be because people who think negatively won't have many memories to look back on or anything they feel passionate about doing... They will live with regrets because they didn't get what they wanted so instead of trying different things out for fun, they just wasted their time thinking, What if? which will never bring them anywhere.
- Negative thoughts increase stress because the part of the brain called the amygdala controls our emotional reactions so if your amygdala decides to convert a stressful event into a memory, then your mind will be in stress mode for the next couple of days or even weeks! So, try not to build up any negative thoughts because that will eventually take its toll on you.

We as people already have a choice as to which mindset we will accept—growth or shrink. When we want to grow, we choose to take things in our stride and handle them the best we can. We use these experiences as lessons that teach us how to be stronger and better at whatever it is we do (ex: the test is an opportunity for you to learn and grow).

When you see things from another angle, knowing that everything happens for your benefit rather than believing it's all random, it helps you through tough times because there's always hope. The energy flowing through you will help you understand why bad things happen so that they don't affect us as much anymore. You know you can bounce back from anything if you just learn from your experiences.

It's all about how you look at things. If you see the glass as half empty, that means everything is terrible and you can't get past it. Sometimes we need that feeling of not being able to get over something so that we don't forget how much it hurts us because this way we won't make the same mistake twice. But if you choose to look at things with a different mindset, seeing the opportunities in every situation, then even if bad things happen to you, they won't affect your life as much.

This way of thinking is gaining more momentum in society today because people are tired of feeling unhappy for no reason when there are better ways of dealing with problems. People see hope in adversity, which allows for new possibilities, opportunities, and ways of thinking to present themselves.

CHANGE YOUR PERSPECTIVE ON THINGS

It's our consciousness that chooses between whether we will grow or shrink. Everything you experience in life can be used for your benefit if you want to use it that way. We all go through difficult times and we can train ourselves to become more resilient so that these times don't define us as much as they used to. It doesn't mean that we learn nothing from those situations, but we learn how to acknowledge what happened and let it go quickly. There's a difference between understanding something vs. letting it play over and over again in your head. If you choose to experience painful situations with this mindset then that means you're allowing yourself to grow because you are learning from those experiences, but if it eats at you, then the pain is only held within, which causes negativity.

The book helps us realize that whenever we think of something as terrible it's because our body reacts by producing the stress hormone cortisol. This hormone is created when we feel threatened. When we think of things as bad, it doesn't allow for positivity to come about since all these negative thoughts block off the energy within us that would otherwise help us let go quickly and carry on with our day. Acknowledging what happened allows for an easier return to a positive state. When we experience something and think about it, the memory is kept in our brain and slowly over time becomes less powerful (if not forgotten). If you keep replaying in your head all the bad things that happened to you then it's like experiencing them for the first time, which makes us feel bad because we haven't allowed ourselves to heal yet. It's by learning from these memories that we move forward and become stronger people because we're no longer afraid of taking on new challenges since we know that if we fail, then there's always next time when we'll be better equipped.

Think about this: You could either choose to hold on to something so tight because you can't let go or you can put it in a rucksack and move forward. It happens that when things are hard for us it's because we're blocking off positivity with all the negative thoughts so it's important to start being more positive about what you're doing even if you don't feel like it, but this way you'll move on faster because you're not letting your mind get in your way.

You can't let go if you keep holding on to something just because it's still part of who you are, but if you acknowledge that this thing is no longer the right path for you then there's nothing holding you back from moving on. If you were to put all these memories into a rucksack then being able to continue with your day without being held back by them would be possible. There's even a parable about this in the book, which shows how life could have been different if people hadn't chosen to hold on to their heavy bags.

If there are problems in your life right now, don't dwell on them so much because it makes them feel insurmountable when they're not. You should learn to acknowledge them, to put them in a rucksack, and move forward because if you don't then your mind will get in the way of your potential growth. If there's something that happened that makes you scared or worried about what might happen then it could be because you're holding on to something that should have disappeared already, which creates negativity inside of you.

Don't let yourself become consumed by fear (this is how people become victims) since all these negative thoughts can make us feel like we're smaller than the problems we face. Don't keep thinking about things too much once they've passed; let them go quickly so that you can carry on with your life without being held back by these memories. Even though it's not easy to acknowledge that these negative things happened, it's better than allowing them to stay because this way you'll be able to move forward.

There are many stories in the book about how people chose to carry on with their lives after painful moments because they recognized that all these bad memories were holding them back. Letting go of these memories allows us to grow as individuals by making sure that we're not restricted or limited at any point during our lives. We all have problems and face challenges so it's important for us to learn how to let go of the past so that we can continue with what happens right now instead of always wondering, What if?

Don't hold on to something just because you think you should since this perception is based on a negative perspective. If you have something in your life that won't help you in the future then it's better to let go of it because holding on to this will block off a better future for you, just like choosing not to forgive someone for doing us wrong is equivalent to allowing them power over our lives.

It's by learning from these memories and changing how we feel about bad things happening to us that we can live more fulfilling lives instead of sitting around waiting for problems to come up (which would only make us feel worse). The book also explains how we can change our perspectives on these memories by giving us examples of stories that show what happens when people don't let go of their negative thoughts and hold on to their pain.

GROWING YOUR SELF-CONFIDENCE AND SELF-ESTEEM

There will be times when you have to go through a lot of pain and suffering, but being able to see the silver lining in these clouds makes it easier.

Bouncier people don't let their negative emotions take over since they're aware that once this happens then they will isolate themselves from the things that would have been good for them, which can create a lot of unnecessary unhappiness. Grit is by itself a very positive thing because it allows people to grow and overcome challenges without getting stuck on problems for too long, which helps them guide their lives towards happiness instead of letting them float wherever life takes them.

People who don't have as much tenacity as they should face a lot of self-doubts because their emotions prevent them from seeing the good things that could come out of different experiences. These people become very unhappy and unfulfilled because they search for happiness in the wrong places, which means that even if something good does happen to them then it won't be satisfying, which is why it's important not to let your negative emotions get control over you since this will only make you feel worse about yourself.

Even though everyone faces challenges at some point or another, resilient people are aware that the way they look at these problems determines how likely they are to succeed or fail. This can help us understand how all of our decisions are based on what we see happening to us and the way we think about these events will have an impact on how successful we are in life.

People who aren't as whippy as they could be let their negative emotions take control of them since they feel that it's better to stay attached to something that makes them unhappy just because it's familiar, even though this generates a lot of unhappiness because being able to move forward is important for everyone.

WHERE IS YOUR FOCUS? IS IT ON THE PROBLEM OR THE SOLUTION?

The idea is to have faith in what you are capable of doing. It's not about giving in to fear all the time but instead learning how to move forward with faith that you can handle whatever comes your way. You are stronger than what you're seeing right now. When you believe this, life becomes easier and more fun because you are making an impact for good.

Whatever happens to you is a gift for learning and moving through something rather than getting stuck by having negative thoughts connected with it. Everything has some kind of connection with something else, so maybe today was meant to happen because of what is going to come tomorrow. Would anyone choose anything that's going to hold them back? No! You can choose to learn from it and move through it.

Life is just the train that we're on and we're all in different cars and compartments of the train: some people are happier than others, some people have more money than others, but your car is still moving forward no matter what. We may be detached from other people because we might feel like they aren't experiencing what we are dealing with, but everyone is doing something so we don't get disconnected from life. It's not a good enough excuse for not taking care of yourself by saying that you're too tired, sick, or busy to take care of yourself. When you neglect yourself, everybody around you feels the effects of it. Nobody wants this because we need each other, especially in times like this.

The world is changing its way of thinking and doing things; people are waking up all over the planet regarding how they relate to life. We're all learning that taking care of yourself first is the number one priority among everything else that comes your way. This means ending relationships that don't work for you, eating healthier food, and staying away from toxic people or environments so you can be happy and healthy. If something doesn't feel right within you then it's time to change whatever thought/action/decision made you feel this way so it won't come back. It's never too late to do anything! You can do anything you want if you have faith in what you are capable of doing. Faith is the result of taking action every day and moving forward because every good thought/action/decision gets us closer to where we need to be. If your car is stuck, then push it out of the mud because everything that happens has a higher purpose.

How much time do we spend talking about all the negative things going on in our world? It's not really about how bad life can be but more importantly how great life can be! We're just too busy focusing on what's wrong when everyone knows there is something much bigger going on here. The whole idea is to wake up from this dream because there will always be negativity when people aren't thinking and acting like they're the ones that create their reality. If you go around thinking that nothing matters then that's what you will get because you are creating this with your thoughts, actions, and beliefs every day.

The power of being human is beyond anything any other species can imagine, but we have to step into our greatness by taking responsibility for how things are in our lives instead of placing blame on someone or something else. That means realizing all of life is a test to see if we are worthy enough to receive more information so we can expand our awareness about everything! We have it within us to be able to do whatever we want because everything has already been done by us before so why not help others remember their greatness too? Do it for yourself and everyone else because we all need you to be the best version of yourself that you can be.

You were created by God/The Universe/Source Energy/ Your Soul, whatever your belief might be. You also have free will and nothing can take that away from you unless you let it. This means nobody has control over what happens in your life no matter who they are or how powerful they think they are. If you sit around thinking that someone else is responsible for everything in your life then this is exactly what will happen because everything begins with a thought, which creates an action then manifests itself into reality. You either win or lose when it comes to making these kinds of decisions so why not win all the time by taking responsibility for everything in your life?

Many of us get caught up in not knowing how to handle certain situations, but this isn't important enough to stop you from taking action. There is always something that we can do if we look deep within ourselves and remember who we truly are. If you're thinking about doing something then go ahead and do it because there is no such thing as a mistake! This doesn't mean running around like a mad person making the same mistakes over and over again; it means taking your mistakes and learning from them so they don't come back and bite you in the butt. Every difficult situation holds some kind of knowledge for us, like when something seems to be too good to be true then it usually is or when someone's reaction doesn't sit well within your stomach then something isn't right. Every situation that we don't like is there to tell us that we need to change our thoughts/actions/decisions so they will never come back and hurt us ever again!

When it comes down to deciding between worrying about what people think of you or doing what feels right within yourself, always choose the latter because this is how we expand our awareness and experiences in every area of life! If we spend most of our time worrying about what other people care about, which is their own lives, then this means we lose focus on who we truly are and what's important here, which happens to be living a life filled with peace and happiness. Nobody can make you happy but yourself and it's our conditioning that keeps us from realizing this fact. The reason why we want others to love us is that we don't love ourselves enough, but this isn't true at all! There is nothing wrong with wanting to be accepted and loved by other people because we do this for ourselves too and if we don't feel like we're good enough then that's exactly what will happen—but it doesn't mean it has to stay this way forever.

Everyone wants to be happy; nobody likes feeling disconnected, unworthy or uninspired, which makes life a lot harder than it really should be! Life should be filled with happiness, peace, and joy all of the time so there is no excuse as to why it shouldn't be this way. If your life isn't what you want it to be, then take full responsibility for the fact that YOU are creating who you are through your thoughts/actions/decisions and nobody else! You can finally stop being a victim of whatever situation has presented itself in your life because you have the power to change all of this with just one thought/action/ decision at a time.

You were born into this world to help others just as much as they were created to help you, so let's learn how to start giving back. After all, when we do, there is no lack or limitation anywhere in our lives anymore because nothing separates us from understanding everything that happens here! We are all connected within our souls so the only reason why we don't feel this connection is because of our fear and resistance against expanding our awareness to a higher level. Every experience that has come into your life so far was created so you could learn from it and use this knowledge as a steppingstone towards expanding your consciousness, which will lead you towards being more comfortable with taking responsibility for every single thing in your life!

This isn't just some technique or method that helps us get by in the material world, but it's a way of evolving into something greater than what we currently are within our souls, which then reflects onto everyone around us. If you want nothing more than to help others then do something about all of these limiting beliefs that keep popping up when they aren't wanted! You were sent here to help others and this starts with yourself because we can only give what we already have and not a penny more.

It's about understanding that every single thing in the world exists as energy and it's our thoughts/actions/ decisions that shape where this energy flows within our lives because everything happens through vibration! If you want something, then simply direct your thought towards having it by sending out a powerful frequency of love, peace, and gratitude, which will evolve into physical reality after crossing over to the other side. We all do this subconsciously, but lately we seem to be forgetting how important it is to remember who we truly are along with why we came here in the first place, which is to expand consciousness onto a higher level.

■ WHAT'S IN IT FOR ME?

The thing about grit is that not only are you becoming more self-aware, but if you can be resilient in your life then this means you will begin to attract more people who want what you have. But when someone comes up against an obstacle and they don't give up, they become stronger. They start attracting positive things in their life because they are holding a space for these positives to come in without the resentment or the victim mentality. This is what tenacity does for you.

You will also become more stylish. You can be resilient about anything and your days will feel good to you! People will want to be around you because they know that, despite whatever happens in their own life, when they are with you it feels good! And how do you get there? By practicing being whippy... If something goes wrong or if someone pushes your buttons don't give up ...just flip the switch and say, "I'm choosing to see this as an opportunity." That's what tenacity is all about.

There are so many people out there who could help us grow but we don't allow ourselves to have mentors or coaches or therapists because of pride...

STOP COMPARING YOURSELF WITH OTHERS – IT'S NOT A COMPETITION!

Don't listen to what anyone else has to say about your life because you are the only one who has a true and honest perspective on your life. You can't compare yourself with someone else because everyone's journey is different!

Everyone here was born from love and they were given a body, mind, and spirit for them to manifest their highest potential, which is why every single human being here holds infinite possibility within them. So why don't most people live out their dreams? Because most of the time they simply give up when something gets hard...

So instead of fighting against these patterns or going down this path, play with it by saying, "Let's see if I can create a greater outcome than this" and, like magic, you will begin to attract whatever it is you want.

The switch of grit comes from understanding that energy cannot be destroyed, it can only change form, which means nothing in your life is ever wasted, it always has the potential to transmute into something more positive if we stop resisting what we don't like and instead accept these obstacles for all that they are, which are opportunities.

CHAPTER 12

ABSOLUTE AND TRUE

We are the determinants of what is "real and true" to us. Statements like, "I've always been...." really end for us in the manner in which we desire. Absolution is a mindset of your choosing that applies to any situation. True grit is built upon absolution.

Resiliency is not about being "tough," it's about the power in developing tenaciousness. It is knowing that everything in your life happens for a reason, even when you don't know what that reason is. Bouncy people are resilient because they have learned to change their reactions, which can turn into habits thereby giving them greater control over their lives. Making purposeful choices that are positive rather than negative changes our stories and, by extension, changes our outcomes.

There are three components of resiliency: character virtues, choice, and knowledge. You may find yourself doing some self-reflection to see how each component relates to you personally.

◼ CHARACTER VIRTUES

A marker of tenacity is having strong character virtues (good moral qualities). Character traits like honesty, courage, patience, and compassion are the foundation upon which you build your life. Honesty means being true to yourself regardless of the consequences. Courage means being true to yourself despite fear. Patience means being patient with others as well as with oneself. Compassion is about having empathy for other people's feelings, needs and experiences so that you can be more understanding towards them rather than judgmental. More importantly, though, it is also about having empathy for yourself so that you can better understand your own needs. It does not mean excusing every bad action you've taken and every bad characteristic trait that you have. It simply means allowing yourself to feel and process negative experiences in a healthy way so that you can move forward rather than reliving the past.

◼ CHOICE

Resiliency is all about choice—we choose what we want our life story to look like. We choose how we interpret the events that happen in our lives, for better or worse. Knowing that everything that happens is for a reason gives you more control over your life because it allows you to reflect on what led up to this event and therefore develop new patterns of behavior so that it does not happen again (see repetition compulsion). So, whenever something goes wrong or there's some adversity, try asking yourself, What am I learning from this? and, What do I need to change in my life so that this won't happen again? This simple practice will save you a lot of suffering because it takes the interpretation away from being something bad or unfair, which can easily lead to you forming lasting beliefs about yourself.

KNOWLEDGE

It's important to be knowledgeable about how events can affect others, especially if that event is connected with oneself. This knowledge helps teach you empathy and understanding of people's feelings and experiences. You can learn about the histories of struggles within various communities around the world and your town so you will better understand why certain things happen and be able to empathize with those affected by these events rather than judging them or becoming angry towards them. Learning the reasons behind why we do what we do helps us be more tolerant of other people, which also makes us less judgmental. It also causes us to think before we speak as well as think before taking action because it gives us a lot more information to base our decisions upon.

THE HOW TO'S OF DEVELOPING YOUR SPIRIT OF RESILIENCY

The first step is to recognize what triggers you, either physically or emotionally, when something bad happens. It can take a while for this awareness to come about because it requires self-reflection. You may have become habituated to having an emotional or physical reaction in certain circumstances without paying much attention to why that is the case. Once you can recognize the triggers it becomes easier for you to choose not to react in that way any longer. The next time that situation comes up, use your knowledge and your choice wisely by choosing how you are going to interpret what's happening rather than following old behavioral patterns simply because they are familiar.

The moment you say something has always been that way, or there was never an alternative, you end your power in the conversation. To be absolute in this sense is not to live life in a dream world but to live in the reality of what can be possible rather than what has always been or will never be. This then permits others to think outside the box as well. The person then opens himself up for new experiences, new ideas, and even new ways of thinking about himself, thus creating growth opportunities.

Absolution allows us to take things personally again, which provides for much greater meaning in our lives because we are not allowing fears to determine what is real rather than what could be possible. This has been one of the greatest blocks of humanity, especially of leaders everywhere—that fear limits who we think we can be and thus limits our journey toward achieving that state.

>Absolution is a mindset of your choosing that applies to any situation.

RESPONSIBILITY

The blame game only takes us so far in getting closer to wherever it is we want to go. The world may even become angry with you at first, but they will get over it quickly when you begin taking responsibility for yourself more than ever before, which makes them more accountable for themselves beyond whatever was done or against you. Once someone realizes they have no control over you, they will be forced to take responsibility for their actions.

This is the measure of a true leader that others will follow. They no longer just simply follow out of fear or obligation but because it has become a habit and there is something about following someone else who takes responsibility despite what they are up against that adds meaning to the journey. The person being followed begins to see more possibilities so therefore understands that taking responsibility can become contagious if one allows it. It becomes an empowering realization on both sides of the aisle, where before there had been nothing but constant struggles due to lack of personal responsibility.

The blame game only takes us so far in getting closer to wherever it is we want to go.

■ THE POWER OF CHOICE

Tenaciousness does not allow for limitations, it thrives on opportunity. We can become victims to our own lives by staying in the situations that are familiar even though they no longer serve us or make us happy. True happiness comes from within and is not something we find outside ourselves because, as stated before, there was never an "out there" but only a perception of what life should be; this is the reality of every human being, regardless of whether they choose to see beyond life as they have known it.

■ SUMMARY

It is time for us all to realize that every person has the opportunity for greatness inside themselves because greatness does not come from external things like money or status but rather an internal burning desire that grows with each obstacle encountered along the journey. We are all capable of this greatness despite who we are or where we are in society today because despite these factors everyone is still an individual with their thoughts and feelings. The greatest step, however, is the first step, which requires tenaciousness to put forth that effort despite whatever form adversity comes in because it is only through adversity that we find out what we are truly made of and who we can be.

CHAPTER 13

YOU CALL THE SHOTS

You decide how life impacts you

How will you show up in your life? Will you start every activity in the manner in which you want to see it end? Start how you want to finish. Start with the expectation that with every peak or valley you will see your finish line come to pass just as you've rehearsed it daily. YOU MUST BECOME THE MASTER OF YOUR LIFE.

You're in charge! YOU are the CEO of your life! YOU call the shots and YOU decide how every situation impacts you. YOU get to choose: will this challenge break or build you? How do you want today to end? If your answer is not with joy, pride and happiness; if it's not filled with inner peace and a sense of satisfaction at having done everything you could, then perhaps you need to make some changes for yourself.

Make the decision now that from here on out, no matter what happens or who tries to tell you otherwise, YOU get to decide how life impacts you...

You have the power to choose how you want every situation in life to impact you. You get to decide: Will this challenge break or build you? Are you going to win today or will it be a day lost? It's your call. Yours is the choice that counts.

Decide TODAY where you want to end up at the end of each day and then commit 100% of yourself into making it happen by taking massive action—start tomorrow with this new mindset and declare out loud, "I am the master of my destiny."

Forget about what others say or think about their experience of your life—you get to choose how every situation impacts you. The high performers I coach and the really smart people too consistently say, "I get to choose."

Forget what other people think about their experience of your life—it's YOUR reality that matters, not theirs!

CREATE A LIST OF THE "RULES" YOU WANT TO LIVE BY

Each day write down 8–10 rules you want to live your life by, such as:

- I don't react, I CHOOSE how I respond.
- When faced with a difficult decision, I ask myself, "What's the worst that could happen?" Then I choose accordingly.

- I embrace change and know that every challenge or roadblock is an opportunity for me to grow.
- I choose to look at my challenges as opportunities for growth, rather than something to beat myself up over.

Repeat these rules out loud first thing in the morning and last thing before you go to bed. Have your family members write their own set of rules too so that it becomes part of your daily routine. It will change your life!

Start taking action towards achieving whatever goal you're after NOW—no matter how little it might be right now, take massive action on that one area right now. The game isn't won on paper; the game is won by making progress today towards the desired result you've established for yourself. No excuses allowed...

You are not a victim of your life, you are a champion of your life, and as such it's up to YOU and only you to make progress towards whatever goal you're chasing; no matter how little that might be right now take massive action on it today.

Remember: You can't change what happened in the past, but you can always choose how every situation impacts you from this day forward! By doing so, no matter what happens or how difficult things might seem, all the power will lie with you and become part of your story....

Don't obsess about what you don't have. Instead, find out what you have right now that the world needs and then give it away; you'll be surprised by how much you receive back!

Your life is a gift to those who follow behind—do not waste it... It's never too late to start living your best life NOW. Take massive action towards achieving whatever goal you're chasing NOW ... no excuses.

YOU are responsible for creating YOUR reality—don't let anyone tell you otherwise.

Say these words aloud daily:

"I get to choose how every situation impacts me."

Take the time to write down exactly what you want out of life—your goals, dreams, and desires ... write them all down. Then go back into each goal and map out how much time it will take for you to achieve each one. Write it down! Be specific, be detailed. When do you expect to have these things attained? What is the first action step that could lead you in that direction? It's never too late or early to make changes today towards whatever goal you're chasing—start TODAY!

Reward yourself for sticking to your set of rules; don't let anyone else decide them for you.

It's your life and you must live according to YOUR rules. Don't let ANYONE else tell you otherwise. At the end of the day, it's only YOU that has to wake up tomorrow and live with yourself... You'll be a lot happier in the long run if you stick with YOUR OWN set of rules instead of someone else telling you how YOU should live.

There is only one way to avoid criticism - do nothing, say nothing, and be nothing.

Don't allow negativity into your life—surround yourself with people who inspire, uplift, and motivate you, they'll make you want to be a better version of yourself. Don't let anyone limit your growth; if someone wants your attention, they've got to put a $1 bill in your hand...You must stay grounded on why success matters and keep living according to those rules.

The key to all success lies within your present moments, the seemingly insignificant daily actions that continue throughout every day. Every second counts. It's never too late or early to make changes today towards whatever goal you're chasing—start TODAY!

DON'T WORRY ABOUT WHAT OTHERS THINK

It's ridiculous how much time we waste worrying about what other people think and the sad part is it truly does matter! What's even sadder than that is the fact that the people we are concerned with have less than you do. We have to decide for ourselves what is important and meaningful to us. The minute you give up on a goal is the minute your subconscious mind gives up. Keep going! Know what you want and take massive action. No matter how small or large it might be, take massive action towards achieving whatever goal you're after NOW.

COMMIT TO YOUR HAPPINESS:

To be happy you have to commit to it. Stop putting it on the back burner just because a lot is going on in your life right now. When things go wrong, when people upset us or hurt our feelings, we don't get mad ... we get better! We move forward from these experiences stronger and more resilient than ever before! You can't hold on to anger and expect happiness. But you also shouldn't let anger control you either. Find a healthy balance of dealing with issues head-on while utilizing positive self-talk to help boost your emotions into a more positive mood.

▐ DEVELOP URGENCY FOR SUCCESS:

You need that drive for success every single day. Think about what you want and feel it. This is where visualization comes in—this is a massively powerful tool to help build your desire for success. Find the time every day to sit down, relax and visualize as much as possible. Imagine yourself achieving those goals, enjoy the moment! Watch as your subconscious mind starts working automatically towards those goals each time you do it.

You have got to believe in yourself if you want others to believe in you. Don't let anyone tell you otherwise!

From now on, any time someone says anything negative or discouraging about YOU, respond with a powerful statement that will shape your mindset into believing more positive things about yourself. If they say, "You'll never change," respond by saying, "I will never quit changing." If they say you are not smart enough, say, "I am determined to figure it out!"

BUILD AN APPETITE FOR LEARNING & DEVELOPMENT

A champion can learn something from everyone. Everyone has something that could teach you about life, about business, about success ... but you won't find out if you don't take the time to ask them how they did it! Don't miss out on that opportunity or experience. Be open-minded and be willing to learn new things every day. That is one of the keys to success in life—being able to do what others can't because you are always looking for ways to improve yourself.

You have got to stop thinking like everyone else! You can't expect to do the same thing that other successful people are doing and expect to get the same results. You have to be willing to learn something new every day, take risks, make mistakes and try new approaches. Be coachable!

FIND WAYS TO MAKE YOURSELF HAPPY REGULARLY

One of the biggest keys to making yourself happy is to find ways to do this regularly. It is very rewarding and fulfilling if you can develop a habit out of doing little things that make you happy regularly. Not only will you be able to create new happiness habits but you'll also help build your tenacity.

Being resilient is being tough, physically or mentally strong enough to recover quickly from difficulties; robust. Developing the ability to bounce back after adversity comes in different forms for everyone; however, there are some commonalities among those who are masters at it. Perhaps one of the most important skills that leaders need to develop today is how they respond during times of stress. It's not about reacting without any foresight but first taking time to recover, make sense of what is happening, gather your thoughts and then respond.

The quote below really summarizes the importance of finding happiness in our lives now instead of waiting until sometime in the future when things are more stable.

"If you wait to be happy until you have solved all the problems that face you this year, you may never be happy. If you can be happy now with no guarantee as to what tomorrow will bring or next week or next month, then when challenges come along in any given year, they do not throw you."

With grit being such an important personal character trait today it only makes sense to focus on developing ways to help us find happiness even when things may be difficult or not going as planned. Here are six ways that you can build happiness habits regularly so you can bounce back faster when adversity strikes.

Perform three random acts of kindness daily

A helpful way to stay happy is to try being nice more often; this will help increase your happiness levels, which then leads to better tenacity. The easiest way to do this is to perform three random acts of kindness daily; you can do this anonymously if you wish by just leaving some money somewhere for example. The main purpose here is that being nice even in small situations will make you feel good and increase your grit at the same time (be sure it doesn't go too far though).

Take some time for yourself daily

Many people neglect their care and wellbeing. We get busy with our daily lives, we do so much and we often forget to stop and take some time for ourselves. We must make room in our schedules each day for a little "me time". This could be practicing yoga or meditation, exercising, or just reading a book. Whatever you can manage that is related to self-care every day will help significantly in making you happier and whippier overall.

Set aside time to dream

While many of us might not feel like we have the luxury of thinking about what we want out of life anymore because everyday life seems to take up all our energy, this habit is still very valuable. It is not only about the big dreams but also about planning out how to achieve them. It can feel very fulfilling to break things down into smaller steps and then create a plan for how these steps can be achieved. Sometimes you need to just brainstorm ideas of what you want your new yearly goals to be.

There are five kinds of dreamers, I am going to share the only one that matters; be the dreamer who:

Dreams big, achieves those dreams, and goes on to dream even bigger dreams!

I'm uncertain if you know this about me, but I've been broke, I know what that life looks and feels like. But here's the reality, broke my friends is a temporary condition. Poor is different. Poor is a state of mind. You see, you can be broke and still be rich in spirit, rich in ambition, rich in courage, rich in determination.

Here is a secret: It costs nothing to dream big, and it costs not a penny more to dream huge.

No matter how broke you might be, the only way you will become poor is by giving up on your dreams.

It's all about a shift in mindset, from "I can't" to "I can"; from beginning at the mercy of circumstance to being at the helm of your life; from being enslaved to being free.

Take time for creativity weekly

Many of us get so bogged down with everyday life that even when we get some free time it's difficult to think creatively. Creativity takes practice so dedicated time spent on something creative each week will help increase this skill along with strengthening the mind in general. If you're having trouble thinking of what could count as creativity, try writing a poem or song lyrics, drawing or painting something, or even doing a jigsaw puzzle.

Keep a gratitude journal

One of the most valuable habits you can have is keeping a list of all the things you are grateful for. This has been shown to have an amazing impact on happiness and wellbeing so it is worth doing this each day, perhaps as soon as you wake up. The simplest way to do it is just journaling what you're grateful for in bullet points or short sentences. Studies have found that those who only write down three things every morning still see major positive changes in their overall mental health from doing this alone!

Make time to exercise daily

The final tip here is to make regular physical activity a part of your everyday routine. By exercising regularly, you will experience a multitude of benefits such as better sleep, reduced stress and anxiety, and improved memory among other things. You could go for a walk each morning or evening before work, you might enjoy taking the stairs at your workplace instead of the elevator and you can even do some stretches while watching TV. The main point here is physical activity requires commitment so be sure to find something that works well with your schedule!

CHAPTER 14

BELIEVE

Believe in yourself and your purpose. This journey and the vision is no one else's, own it. Visualize even if just for a few minutes at the start of your day and a few at the end. Our psychology is the biggest hurdle, not making the money or getting the relationship of our dreams but rather believing we deserve these things is the hardest part.

The biggest hire you will make is yourself, your belief in yourself. Find strength from within and own it and use it every day. It is the difference between failure and success, stagnation and growth, victimization and victory. We all have unique gifts that we give to the world when we share them with freedom and responsibility. When we hold back on our unique gifts, we limit ourselves and fall into smallness or, worse yet, misery, desperation, and dependency on others because deep down inside we do not feel worthy of greatness.

Believe in your potential power to contribute by trusting your gut, making decisions through focusing on the outcome desired rather than worrying about whether or not you can do something or what others think of you. Use affirmations daily to develop a self-image that is consistent with the reality you desire. Affirmations are not just positive thinking, but they are focused attention to create a certain outcome. I'm sure you have heard before about repetition being the mother of skill; well, this is part of it, what you focus your attention on grows and develops into a thought habit or a belief system. The more we do something the better we get at it, affirmations work in this same way whether they are conscious or subconscious thoughts.

We must believe in our inherently powerful ability to contribute by joining together and using the power of teamwork through synergy. Synergy happens when people come together for a common purpose and everyone involved gives up their independence for interdependence, this creates a whole that is stronger than the individual parts. When you are dedicated to your purpose and passionate about your mission, working with other people who have similar goals this process happens naturally.

Our attitude affects our performance so take care of it through positive thought and behavior because we all have a choice in how we respond to any situation or person even if not initially. With choice comes responsibility so own every action you take every day instead of blaming someone else for what has happened; learn from it and move forward into possibility. Remember each one of us is blessed with unique talents that can make an impact on our world when put into service through these gifts by loving unconditionally rather than judging conditionally causing separation between us as human beings versus connection, which is what we are here for.

Believe in your power to contribute no matter what the situation is by acting with authenticity and living in integrity. Authenticity means being true to yourself rather than putting on a mask to fit in or fool others. Integrity is our ability to link our beliefs, values, and behaviors so they are consistent. Acting with authenticity doesn't mean you will never be nervous again or always feel spontaneous joy but that you act from your true authentic self, not just when it is convenient but all of the time because it feels right. Sometimes this means doing what might not be popular or even comfortable to maintain your sense of self while helping others with empathy instead of sympathy or judgment.

You must believe in yourself and your power to contribute no matter what the situation is by promoting harmony and balance in your life. Harmony and balance are achieved when you take time for yourself, developing a structure that works for you versus around you. You need downtime away from stress; this is not laziness but the ability to refresh the mind through things like meditation or yoga, which allows us to become well-rounded instead of one-dimensional people who burn out because they don't understand how to manage themselves appropriately. Living in the moment allows us to embrace our spontaneity too instead of always living in our heads worried about future possibilities.

Believe in your potential power to contribute by staying focused on what matters most rather than being distracted all of the time. Make it a point not to participate or even speak in gossip, being distracted with things that don't matter will never help you achieve your goals. Keep yourself accountable by making choices that are best for you instead of succumbing to peer pressure or what others want you to do just because they are doing it. Keeping up with social media is fine but set limits so you are not constantly online versus living life in reality without feeling overwhelmed.

Be willing to trust yourself enough to take the next step knowing the only way to get where you want to go is if the change is necessary; it may be uncomfortable at first but taking risks keeps your life alive and brings newness into your world daily. This takes courage, which is the ability to face fear and move forward anyway so you can grow. You will be scared at first but you have a soul that is longing for growth and this process is what allows us to become the best self we can be no matter how many times we stumble along the way.

Be willing to trust others enough too by being transparent with everyone in your life versus keeping things locked up inside until it becomes an issue that explodes later on after you have lost important relationships.

Trusting people means providing them with the information they need to make good decisions based on all of the facts instead of withholding certain pieces because it makes you look or feel better; this creates mistrust, which causes problems in all types of relationships including family, friends, and professional working environments.

When you trust yourself and others, your power to contribute blossoms; embracing your true self by leading with authenticity instead of always putting on a mask is the key. This allows you to be comfortable in your skin while being accountable for what you say or do. You are more focused on outcomes that truly matter because you have taken time for yourself through activities that bring balance into your life versus always living in crisis mode.

Living authentically empowers you to take risks making more conscious choices so the outcome is better rather than coming up short due to distraction or lack of courage, which can hinder living according to plan. Trusting people means being transparent so all involved know what is expected of them without any mixed messages leaving room for misinterpretation, which leads to confusion and chaos versus clarity and understanding.

When you trust yourself and others, your power to contribute grows exponentially. After all, you know where to focus your energy towards making choices that create harmony and balance for all of those around you instead of feeling like a victim because everything doesn't go as planned all of the time. This is not giving up on reaching your goals but simply shifting gears into a more focused plan that works with what you already have going on at that moment in time, which is what grit is really about.

Do not be afraid to change direction when needed so you can meet these goals with confidence because living authentically allows for this flexibility instead of being one-dimensional versus boring. This inspires others around you, helping them see their full potential instead of playing small, which is a disservice to those around you. Being whippy means knowing when and where to do what it takes for all involved to end up in a better place versus staying stuck in the mud.

Many people spend their lives looking backward, dwelling on what did not happen versus asking themselves what is next that will bring them closer to their goal. Living authentically allows for this flexibility by maintaining balance in all things, living with both feet on the ground while having faith in reaching your ultimate destiny.

Live life according to plan, which means knowing where you are going versus being led off track by empathetic individuals versus understanding how it feels to be you versus taking responsibility for the choices they make, which includes hurting others along the way because of neglect or ignorance. Tenaciousness does not mean putting up with this behavior but standing strong in knowing that when people hurt us, we have a choice in deciding if we want to sink into victim mode, blocking our happiness, or stand tall and hold our heads high because we know we did our best, which is all we can ask for in this world called Earth where chaos and confusion reign supreme versus clarity and understanding.

CHAPTER 15

REWRITE YOUR STORY

Write your new story

Ask yourself, "Who am I"?

You are who you believe yourself to be. In the end, you are the story you tell about yourself.

*If you want to change your life, you must change the story you tell about yourself.

*If you want to change your marriage, you must change the story you tell about your marriage

*If you want to change your business, you must change the story you tell about your business.

*If you want to change your body, you must change the story you tell about your body.

You are who you believe yourself to be, driven by your stories!

Sit down and write out your story as you plan to have it come to be. Take your time and write it without limit. Go deep and be outrageous. Your story can be fantastical and as you're writing repeat to yourself, "As I believe so it is granted unto me."

Write about how you are resilient and don't give up. Write about what you want your life to be like.

The mind tends to stop taking in information that is not helpful and this exercise will help empower the new story and keep it fresh in your mind.

When you find yourself thinking about old limits or times when you felt stuck, I suggest repeating, "I am now creating my reality according to my desires." You can also repeat, "I love myself as much as I love others."

REFLECT ON YOUR PAST – EXPAND YOUR STORY TO INCLUDE EVERYTHING

Who have you been in the past? Who were you before this situation, before this relationship, and before these thoughts? Who are you now? What will you be in the future when all of these things change for the better?

Take a good look at who you were to see how far you have come. Try not to focus on where others might think you could have done better or why it was not good enough.

Focus instead on your growth.

Remember that who we are is made up of our history, but it doesn't define us.

Cherish who you were and what has happened to better know yourself and your story.

REMIND YOURSELF OF HOW FAR YOU'VE COME – REMIND YOURSELF DAILY

Despite where we may feel we are, there is always good news in the growth we have experienced. Whenever we begin laboring under a cloud of perceived failures or mistakes, it's important to remember that we have grown in ways that will serve us in the future and these successes and moments of clarity. Memory is just an emotional perception that our brain uses to filter information, so when you want to put things into perspective try to reflect on when you felt happy because at one point this was something new for you too.

WRITE ABOUT THE FUTURE YOU WANT TO CREATE FOR YOURSELF

When you get up in the morning, take an hour to write down your goals for the day, but split them into smaller steps so that it seems more manageable. Then move on to this evening and then tomorrow morning. You'll find that achieving each goal becomes easier because you're getting closer to what you want out of life. And once one thing is achieved it will give you more confidence for the next step forward because there is something already accomplished behind you to build on!

It was not until I started using affirmations (writing my future) rather than resolutions (vowing to make changes) that I saw any kind of positive change in my life because it gave me a sense of purpose, something worth working towards. And when you have a goal, it's important to remind yourself of it every day so that your mind doesn't forget what it is you are working towards.

I hear all the time about how people set goals but never reach them. But if you don't write down these goals and put them somewhere where you can see them every day (like on your PC desktop) then they might as well not exist. I would recommend starting each day with an affirmation or, even better yet, something written in the present tense like, "I am already successful; I am already rich; I am already healthy..." Then go into more detail such as, "Now that I make $100K/year, I am going to buy a big house," and continue until you reach your ultimate goal. If it helps you, go in order backward from the end goal to the middle steps in between.

But if you want a real shot at getting somewhere with this, get yourself a small stack of index cards and write down everything about your future self that you wish to be. For example, "I am healthy; I get up early every day and work out before work; I get promoted by the company so that my salary is increased every year; I eat right and take time for fun too."

After writing down all these benefits of reaching the goal, write down why you desire them. "I want to be healthy because I want to be around my future family; I want to get promoted so that others can look up to me and aspire to do what I've done; I want to maintain a good salary (enough for the lifestyle I desire) so that I don't have to worry about money anymore."

And then next put down all the obstacles that might prevent you from achieving them: "I am not motivated in getting up early and working out" (obstacle); "I will start slow and gradually work into it" (remedy). And then brainstorm ways of looking at things differently so you can overcome these obstacles—try putting yourself in the mind frame of someone who has already achieved this goal. For example: "I am a morning person because I have to be at work early and not sleeping in will give me more time off over the weekends."

This is the kind of daydreaming that artists do when they're painting a picture or someone passionate about something does when they are writing their next article. Instead of being so serious all the time, take some time out for yourself to daydream about what you want your future to look like. And remember this: thoughts become things so if you can see it happening, there's a higher chance of making it happen!

And if we never carried on with these aspirations, we would never find out what we could achieve—we may only discover our limits and possibilities by taking chances and seeing where it takes us.

As they say, "Fall seven times, stand up eight." We've all been through those hard times where everything seems to be going wrong and it's easy to give up on your dreams but those who don't give up are those who succeed—those who persevere.

So remember not to look at life as a series of problems and obstacles but instead as opportunities for greatness and new beginnings.

CHAPTER 16

EMPOWER SPEECH

Self-talk. From this point on we will only use powerful, empowering speech in our daily lives. Any statement after "I am" is only that which we want to see come to pass. Instead of "I am broke" we'll communicate "I am wealthy in many ways." Instead of "I am a failure" we'll say, "I have many successes that I have yet to accomplish." Instead of being a colloquial negative nelly, we'll indulge in the richness of a vibrant language. Instead of "I am depressed" we'll say, "I am overflowing with enthusiasm and optimism." Instead of anything short of greatness, we shall declare our mastery over circumstances that would otherwise cramp our style.

Self-talk is an important aspect of developing our sense of tenacity because it allows us to focus on positive aspects of life instead of negative. We may often put ourselves down, calling ourselves names or focusing only on the bad aspects in our lives rather than all that we have accomplished or will accomplish. Self-talk gives us a place we can go to when we are feeling down and remind ourselves why we need not be down any longer. Keeping a positive attitude in whatever situation will allow us to keep moving forward towards our goals, rather than falling into a state of depression or otherwise negative mindset.

Believe in yourself—then believe even more so. We often feel powerless because we don't put enough faith in ourselves and what we are capable of doing. If you need to lose weight, do not say, "I'll never be thin enough to wear that dress again." Instead, say, "I am re-energizing my body with fresh fruit and vegetables every day until I look better than I ever have before." The first statement is an expression of despair while the second statement gives us something to chew on for motivation. When you empower your speech, everything changes! What will come out of our mouths will only be that which we want to see materialize. It takes practice and staying conscious in the present moment, but it is possible with a little diligence.

Self-talk indicates what we believe about ourselves to be true while empowering speech is another way of saying that we are capable of doing something and will do it (perhaps even despite how we feel). Believing in our capability is what keeps us moving forward when things get difficult, especially when we lose sight of why we started doing something in the first place.

Instead of losing confidence over what may seem like an insurmountable obstacle to overcome, believing that you can achieve your goal regardless helps ensure that you'll never give up on yourself or your dream.

The more we communicate positively the more we program our brains for success.

Unhelpful self-talk. This is a lot of "I can't" and "I should have." It's putting myself down or saying that I can't do something when in fact I have been able to do it. It's comparing myself to others and saying I'm not good enough, pretty enough, or thin enough. The disempowering speech will cripple our efforts and diminish the meaning we hold of ourselves.

▌ SELF-AFFIRMATION

Affirmation is a positive belief about ourselves, an expression of our values, and a way to improve how we feel. Our self-beliefs influence the gap between our perceived self-worth and our actual self-worth. Writing down messages daily is one way to help increase the success gap so that we grow in size instead of shrinking.

Self-affirmation. This is the process of reminding ourselves of our good qualities and gaining confidence in our ability to succeed at tasks we find difficult. It can be helpful when we're faced with a potentially threatening situation such as an interview, public speech, or social encounter and it helps us cope and perform better than we normally would.

It frees up cognitive resources that could otherwise be consumed by worry and forces us to focus on the task at hand rather than the situations surrounding it.

THE POWER OF SPEECH

The power of speech is indeed great. The words that we speak, or share in any form, manifest into our lives just as they are seeded into the world. If you're speaking negatively to yourself, you'll begin to see failures and losses crop up more frequently throughout your day. This negative self-talk will perpetuate itself until it becomes a condition of your being.

To avoid this predicament, simply focus on what you want rather than what you don't want. When you catch yourself starting down a negative path, catch it immediately and redirect those thoughts towards something positive, if not for your sake then for those around you who may be exposed to your toxic language as well as for those whose lives have been or will be affected by the things you're saying to yourself.

You can still vehemently disagree with people, what you can't do is counteract their words with negative speech directed at them. This makes all forms of discourse useless as you become a hostile person unwilling to engage in civil conversation. If someone says something that you don't agree with, just embrace it for what it is … their opinion or view of the world, which deserves respect just like yours does.

EMPOWERING BELIEFS

A paradigm shift has occurred where you now acknowledge that there are no failures only feedback; therefore, mistakes are nothing more than opportunities to grow. The more you acknowledge this the less of a sting failure will have on your emotional status. One of the most powerful things you can do to empower yourself is to develop a growth mindset rather than a fixed one. In other words, don't think that your talents and abilities are set in stone but instead recognize that they have room for improvement and that with effort they can be expanded upon.

◼ HOW TO EMPOWER YOUR VOICE

When you speak, the words that come out of your mouth are intended to empower or disempower. Some people have voices that speak loud and clear while others have muted tones that only create confusion for those who hear them. To develop a voice worth listening to, practice speaking with clarity so others can easily understand what you're communicating. There is no excuse for mumbling under your breath.

Another aspect of developing a strong voice is realizing how much power our external situations hold over us. If we're constantly in environments filled with negativity, whether it comes from friends, co-workers, family members, or strangers, we will eventually take their words to heart and it will begin to disempower us. If we cut the ties to negative people, we gradually start empowering ourselves because we no longer allow their words and actions to infect our spirit and steal our joy!

The third aspect of developing a strong voice is speaking without bragging or boasting. There's a huge difference between proudly offering information about yourself and braggadocios behavior that demeans others in the process, repeatedly putting oneself above everyone else. Instead of speaking with conceit, speak from your accomplishments using "I" statements such as, "I made three sales today; I completed this project ahead of schedule; I was elected secretary for my club," leaving out phrases like, "I'm the best, I'm the greatest, I'm the only one who can…"

As you develop your voice and empower it to put positive vibes into the environment wherever you go, enjoy how people begin rallying around you as they feel empowered by your speaking ability—a beautiful circle of life!

CHAPTER 17

STRENGTH ASSOCIATIONS

Anchors – Dialectical behavior
therapy, nonjudgment.

It is by contrast that our desires are affirmed. We appreciate light after darkness and abundance after times of lack. We are attracted to the brightest star in the sky. The darkest hour of the night is when our spirit is most easily crushed by difficulties and leads us to doubt ourselves, but it is also at this time that we must remember who we are and make a choice not to be overcome by adversity. There is power in developing a spirit of tenaciousness, recognizing what your standards are for yourself, having an anchor during difficulty to help you gain clarity on how to proceed.

Everyone's weaknesses and difficulties are different; some may fall apart during times of conflict and others may respond with anger. Some people need alone time to reflect and seek peace while others need a distraction and require activity. Your friends and family may be able to identify what your vulnerabilities, triggers, and coping mechanisms are by observing your emotional state. They will have more clarity on how you best receive help from them knowing this information about you.

Bear in mind that everyone is capable of developing grit. If you can accomplish this, it means that you possess the power to create your destiny. It is remaining calm and maintaining your standards for yourself in times of chaos that will allow you the best chance at success in reaching your goals.

Building strength associations will help with any self-esteem issues, anxiety disorders, panic attacks (including agoraphobia), post-traumatic stress disorder (PTSD), obsessive-compulsive disorder (OCD), or emotional problems resulting from past trauma.

Developing resiliency is also about reducing conflict with others; interpersonal difficulties may include difficulty with conflict resolution, difficulty understanding how to express yourself under stress, or difficulty caring for your health.

Before a crisis – Remembering love, freedom, choice/ ability to choose, or resourcefulness.

During a crisis – Self-soothing, slowing down thoughts, practicing patience with others/self/circumstances.

After a crisis – Reflecting on what has been learned from the experience and how you are stronger because of it. Using mindfulness to focus on the present moment and be aware of the change.

CONCLUSION

There's power in the singularity of focus. Run your race. Win for the sake of turning your story around. If you want to win at the expense of someone else losing, you've already looked away from the finish line and put your attention on the other runner. You've already lost focus. For the sake of a singularity of focus, you have to maintain your attention on the finish line. If that means you have an uncomfortable moment or two while jockeying for position, so be it. Everyone wants to chase success. I suggest you chase discomfort. Being uncomfortable translates to growth occurring.

I hope through my trials and tribulations I can help people realize there's nothing wrong with being knocked down but if they stay down too long, they expose themselves to becoming completely irrelevant. I am a living testament of what happens when a person chooses not to let a bad break define them; it determines how they respond. It defines their tenacity and ability to find redemption within them. If you stay down too long it might be best for everyone if you just lie there because nobody wants to help someone who doesn't want to help themselves. If you stay down, don't be surprised if people start treating you like a doormat or dirt they can walk all over or throw in their backyard like an old towel that needs replacing.

To find redemption within yourself sometimes one of your greatest strengths can also be your greatest weakness. Intensity is good but when you let your intensity get out of control it can be deadly. Sometimes you become so focused on what you want to accomplish and how you're going to do it that you fail to recognize the subtle signals life sends. You might even choose to ignore those signals and go against them because they don't fit into your plan.

Well, wake up! Life doesn't just happen around us; we are a part of it too. We have our plans but sometimes we need help from outside forces or triggers that will redirect us just long enough for us to refocus on where we want to go. It is only when we collide with those outside forces that we realize this isn't about us at all; it's about the journey itself.

It is not always about reaching the destination but rather enjoying the journey. And sometimes, when you're in that moment of suffering and despair, there might be nothing more important than that one word: resiliency. Tenaciousness is what allows us to see ourselves for who we are today. It takes our mistakes, heartbreaks, failures, and even tragedies and uses them as fuel for change because grit chooses to make its changes within before anybody or anything can do it for you. You have to want it deep down inside before anyone else can give it to you ... and once you decide, don't let go! Sometimes those moments hurt so badly all they will allow you to do is take a breath and realize you're still alive.

Life doesn't always go according to plan; we've all heard that before, but what happens when it never goes as you imagined? What happens when all those big dreams and small accomplishments just fade away? The challenge of resiliency is not only to find the strength within you to fight back but also to find the reason why even with those disappointments and setbacks, those struggles, or those seemingly insurmountable odds ... why should any of us ever stop believing in ourselves and our ability to overcome? It takes conscious effort and an unwillingness to give up.

ABOUT THE
AUTHOR

Shaun L. Murphy, M. Ed., known as Mister Motivation, is a transformative force in the world of motivational speaking and music. An Army Veteran and dedicated educator, Shaun has committed his life to combatting the scarcity mindset and empowering military veterans, youth, and adults to unleash their maximum potential. As the founder of Wake The Beast, Inc., he has created a movement that blends powerful motivational messages with dynamic musical performances, turning pain into power and purpose.

Welcome to the Breakthrough Bunker, where Shaun leads a tribe of relentless warriors dedicated to shattering every limit in their path. Here, excuses are the enemy, and mediocrity is a sin. Shaun's unwavering commitment to personal and professional development is evident in his roles as a devoted husband, father, and active community member. If you're ready to abandon your comfort zone, embrace the grind, and redefine what it means to truly live, join Shaun on a journey that will ignite the fire within you and transform your life. Discover the profound impact of a man who turns struggles into strengths and challenges into triumphs, and be inspired to learn more about his powerful mission.

Shaun is a Motivational EDU-tainer!

Author | Speaker | Musician | Entrepreneur
Spoken Word Artist |Peak Performance Life Coach

He invites you to visit his websites:

www.wakethebeast.org
www.mister-motivation.com

Also by
Shaun L. Murphy

The Amazon best seller *Prompt Journal* is designed to help individuals from all walks of life reflect on their past, embrace their present circumstances, and design their future using the transformative 5M framework of Mindset, Motivation, Money, Management, and Massive Movement.